WHAT IS A MANAGER?

EFFECTIVE MANAGEMENT SKILLS

WHAT IS A MANAGER?

JOHN SCOTT &
ARTHUR ROCHESTER

Sphere/British Institute of Management

First published by
Sphere Books Ltd/BIM 1984

Copyright © Harper Scott Limited

Typeset by H.M. Repros, Glasgow.
Printed and bound in Great Britain by
Cox & Wyman Ltd, Reading

Cartoons by Paula Youens
End of Chapter patterns by John Plumb

Contents

Preliminaries

There's got to be a reason for adding to the mountain of books about management. Several reasons in fact.

One reason: despite that mountain, there's still a shortage of books that deal with the guts of the management job. Most of them take a particular angle — usually business management, sometimes public administration, and then there's a further narrowing of the target area to production or marketing or finance or office management or whatever. This makes them a bit too specialised for anyone who's looking for the basic essentials of what management itself is about (as opposed to other sorts of occupation), what a manager does, the way he thinks, the kind of skills and habits he needs to develop as a 'good manager'.

Another reason: the books that do take the broad view are mostly fairly sophisticated. They're written, consciously or unconsciously, for the middle to upper levels of the management spectrum. But the mass of people in management jobs are at the lower levels of the spectrum, and they find it a bit difficult to translate the concepts they're offered into practical ideas they can actually use in their own jobs. Judging by the things that go on inside many organisations, even people at higher levels find it difficult too.

Yet another reason: a lot of the stuff really is heavy reading. From the authors' point of view this must limit their market. More seriously, from the potential readers' point of view it cuts them off from a wealth of good advice. Most people just won't read stuff they find difficult and dull.

So what we're trying to do in this book and the others in the series is to put together a view of management that is coherent, that makes practical sense, and that is easy to assimilate. If in the process we touch some sensitive nerves among the management ranks, so much the better. Too much so-called 'management thinking' is woolly, conventional and complacent. Perhaps that's why there is so much bad management about.

One practical problem we've had is to do with sex. That's not what you might be thinking. It's simply that a lot of managers are women, but to keep the style of writing simple you've got to choose your pronoun. Do you call a manager 'him' or 'her'? We offer our apologies to all the she-managers we might have insulted, but we've opted for 'him' pretty well throughout. Please take this as a problem of language, not an attempt to cut half the human species out of management.

Before you read on, try this quiz on the subject of managers and management. It's intended to get you thinking about some of your basic assumptions, and about the kinds of terms that are part of the common currency of talk about management. Choose which of the three answers to each question you find it easiest to agree with. You may feel that in different circumstances different answers are right, but which seem to be the best in a general sense? Later on you'll be able to look back at your choices to see if you'd still make them the same way.

Management quiz

1. Who qualifies for the description 'manager'?
   a) Anyone who has other people reporting to him in an organisation, whether he is the chief executive or a supervisor.
   b) Everyone above the supervisory level who has management or executive status.
   c) Only those whose job-titles include the word 'manager'.

2. Which attribute does a manager need most to enable him to 'manage'?
   a) Superior expertise in the work done by his subordinates, the ability to do the more difficult things himself.
   b) Superior skill in organising and motivating his subordinates to do the work, not necessarily a superior expertise himself in the work.
   c) A strong personality and high intelligence.

3. If a manager makes a bad decision, which is likely to do the most damage?
   a) A bad decision about how to get an important operational task done.
   b) A bad decision about buying an expensive piece of equipment.
   c) A bad decision about promoting someone.

4. How well ought a manager to understand financial matters?
   a) Not much — that's what the accountants are there for. His job is to get things done, not to worry about money.
   b) Quite well. He has the real responsibility for the money tied up in his operation, not the accountants.
   c) It all depends. If he's managing a commercial function he does need some understanding, but probably not if he's in (say) a production function or a public service.

5. Is there any essential difference between management and administration?
   a) No, not really. They're both much the same kind of job.
   b) It's a question of the kind of organisation one is talking about. An administrator is a manager in a public body like a hospital or local government department.
   c) There's a very big difference between them, whatever kinds of organisation they're done in.

6. Is a manager a type of businessman, or a businessman a type of manager?
   a) Neither. The two of them need very different kinds of abilities.
   b) A manager in a profit-making enterprise has to be a businessman.
   c) There's no difference. Anyone who's a good businessman is a good manager.

7. What best shows a manager to be a 'good delegator'?
   a) The fact that he has cleared his own job of all the less important chores and routines.
   b) The fact that his subordinates get explicit instructions for each task that he delegates?
   c) The fact that he keeps himself informed about how his subordinates are using whatever freedom of action he has delegated to them.

8. What does planning mean for a manager?
   a) It's an important activity in every manager's job, and one he should try to find time for.
   b) It's not a separate activity. It's a skill he ought to apply in almost everything he does.
   c) It's an important part of some managers' jobs. Other managers have hardly any scope to do it at all.

9. Should a manager try to improve his people's abilities?
   a) Yes, he can do a lot to help them improve their performance in the work they're doing.
   b) No. That's a job for skilled trainers. He shouldn't interfere with their responsibility.
   c) No. They learn by experience, not by anything their manager does to them.

10. A manager needs commonsense and the ability to think. But can he do anything to improve his thinking powers?
    a) No. They depend on his basic intelligence and he can't change that.
    b) Not much. It's mainly a matter of how well he has been educated.
    c) Yes. Thinking is a skill that he can develop if he perseveres.

1. The muddle about management

Probably you're reading this book because you either are, or hope to become, a manager. Possibly, though, it's because you're not really sure whether you're a manager or not — and it would be nice to know. So how do you tell? Do you have to be *called* a manager, or have a 'management' position? Or is it enough to have a job in which you *act* like a manager? Anyway, how do managers act?

Suppose you're a fairly young man or woman, in your twenties perhaps. For some years you've been working in an organisation. The kind of outfit doesn't matter for the moment, nor its size come to that. Small firm, biggish company, huge corporation. Fifty employees or fifty thousand. It could be an arm of government — a local authority operation or ministry department. The one thing that does matter here is that it's an *organisation*, a pile of people doing jobs at different levels. At the top are people making decisions; at the bottom, you and all the

1

other folk who actually do the various things the organisation exists to do.

The job you've been doing there might be almost anything. But one thing you can say with absolute certainty is that it hasn't been a management job. Perhaps you've been an office or production worker, a technician or an accountant, a salesperson or a local government employee. Whatever the job, you know you were at the bottom of the pile. But you worked hard, did the job well and took some pride in it.

So they decided to promote you. Now you're in charge of other people. You're their superior and have the right to give them orders. You can make up your mind about things that previously you just had to accept. But you don't have a completely free hand — you've also got a boss (who might or might not be called a manager), and *he* in turn reports to someone even higher up the pile. Right at the top is a collection of people you all call 'The Management' or something similar, although most of them aren't actually called managers. They have titles such as Directors or Controllers or Executives or Chief Officers. They are the real power in the pile and everyone watches their step when they're about.

Back to the question: are you a manager *now*? They don't call you a manager of course. You're a supervisor or section leader or something lke that. Can you be a manager if you don't have the word 'manager' in your job title? What about your boss? Or is it only people who are part of the Management who are managers? What does 'managing' mean anyway?

It's not surprising if you're confused. Most of us are, and who can blame us? If we're customers of an organisation, the pushy ones among us know that we're more likely to get some action about our complaints of poor service or faulty goods if we insist on 'speaking to the manager' — and refuse to be fobbed off with a mere supervisor or some other obviously non-managerial type. Newspapermen and television reporters use the same idea if they get wind of a nasty cock-up in a public body. They insist on 'speaking to the manager' too — some high-ranking individual they can later pillory for his failure to act (or more often for his ignorance of what was going on). But this doesn't prove any general agreement on what managers are or what they do — apart from having the power to throw their weight about inside their organisation. Companies themselves often muddy the water by giving imposing titles to relatively junior positions. Perhaps they're trying to impress the people in them with their importance in the scheme of things. Perhaps they're trying to impress the public who have contact with their people.

Confused outsiders wouldn't really matter. But confused insiders *do* matter. Most of the troubles in our organisations start from misunderstandings about what 'managing' means and from failures to think out what abilities it needs. They're the fault of 'Managements' who don't manage. They're the fault of 'Managements' who don't require their managers to act like managers. They're the fault of managers who don't act like managers because they don't *think* like managers. They're the fault of people in management jobs who don't see themselves as managers and so don't manage in any real sense.

Just consider your own experiences at work. The chaos caused by 'managers' interfering with things their staff were perfectly competent to do. The anxieties and low morale caused by 'managers' leaving their people in the dark. The inertia caused by 'managers' ducking necessary decisions for the sake of a quiet life. The frustrations caused by 'managers' ignoring the difficulties their subordinates are trying to cope with. The waste caused by 'managers' dodging their clear responsibility to tackle problems in their organisations.

Then look around you to what you know goes on elsewhere and at more senior levels. Boards of directors whose gross mismanagement is revealed to have brought their companies to the brink of collapse. Top executives whose attempts to gag critics of their organisations' waste and incompetence are publicly exposed. School heads and hospital administrators whose establishments have become public scandals. A civil service that is publicly castigated for being almost totally unmanaged.

And then suspect what goes on out of sight. For every well-publicised major foul-up that has cost a company or the tax-payer several millions, there are countless expensive nonsenses that have been kept well hidden. The waste adds up to many hundreds of millions every year. And most of them are, in one way or another, failures of *management*. If the average competence of surgeons were as low as the average competence of managers, the death rate on operating tables would turn hospitals into morgues.

There are many reasons for this fine mess. But most of them spring from a couple of widely-held assumptions about management. In themselves they aren't exactly false ideas, in fact they're hardly ideas at all in any conscious sense. They are more a kind of management folklore — notions so deeply embedded in our thinking that we're hardly aware of them. The danger lies in the wrong ideas they put into managers' heads about who they are and how they ought to think and act.

3

The first is the notion that anyone in management occupies a position of status and power in his organisation. This predisposes those who think of themselves as managers to regard management as something they *are* rather than as a job to do. If they did nothing, they'd still be managers. Some seem to take it as a license to indulge in political games to protect or enhance their status and self-importance. Even more damaging is the way the notion causes them to ignore or disparage the efforts of those at the supervisory level who do try to do a good management job.

The second notion follows on from the first. It is that the position automatically bestows on those who reach it the ability to handle its demands. To get into management you first prove yourself a good worker. It's true you can also get there by string-pulling or being the chairman's son, but that's generally regarded as cheating. The proper way is to get yourself some experience at the bottom of the ladder. If you become good at your job there, you're due for promotion. Promotion eventually gives you the status and power that enables you to 'manage'. The idea is that management is a rank that's earned by time-serving.

There is a third notion that's different from the other two. It's less widely held but often forms a basis for the 'high-flyer' philosophy which works on the principle of spotting the young men (rarely women) who are presentable, intelligent and ambitious, and then carefully grooming them for management. The notion is that management is really a bag of rather specialised and clever tricks. If you're expert in the techniques of things like marketing and finance and are good with figures and can talk knowledgeably about 'Transactional Analysis' and 'Quality Circles' or whatever the latest fads are, then you've got the qualifications for management. Never mind if you're a bit short on such old-fashioned qualities as integrity, common-sense, level-headedness and all the down-to-earth practical abilities that are the bedrock of good management.

The cause of most of the things that go wrong inside organisations (and that aren't sheer bad luck) is a manager's failure to do something that he should have done, or his failure to do it right. It's often quite a simple basic failure. And its cause is often that at the time he was concentrating on something else that was less important. But trace the causes back to their roots and you'll find them embedded in someone's mistaken ideas about what management really means. That someone might be the manager who has failed. Most often though, he's only accepting the ideas of the people who surround him. And *they've* had their wrong ideas confirmed by the knowledge that everyone else thinks the same way. But because ideas are widely held doesn't necessarily make them right.

Once upon a time, nearly everyone assumed the earth was flat. The very fact that the idea was so generally accepted was enough to keep other possibilities out of people's minds. Those few people who did think differently were ridiculed or ignored. Clearly they were wrong because everyone said so. It wasn't until enough people actually tried operating on a different assumption — that the earth was round — and proved it worked, that the old idea finally died.

Today's popular notions of management have much the same effect as the flat earth belief. Too few people realise how much effect these notions have in creating the bad management that's so widespread. Of course there *are* well-managed organisations. There are well-managed *departments* in organisations that are otherwise badly managed. But poor management is the norm, and the popular notions encourage poor managers to go on as they are. This won't change until we have at all levels in our organisations enough managers who operate on the equivalent of round-earth principles — who understand what management really is and who are prepared to act on that understanding.

Chapter summaries

We are going to summarise each main section of the book with a pattern — a visual way of putting together the main points we've covered. The idea is to make it easier to recall what you've just read. We remember things more easily is we can visualise them somehow.

Overleaf is a pattern for the first chapter.

The muddle about management

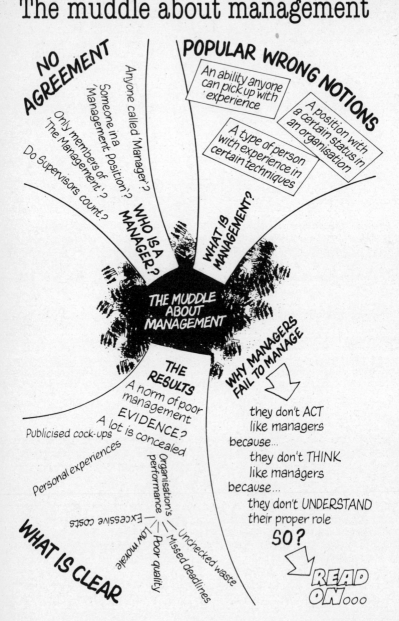

2. What management isn't

One way to try to clarify what we mean by 'managers' is to produce a definition of their function. Take that very simple definition that's been around since God-knows-when:

'Managers get things done through other people'.

That is all right as far as it goes. It does suggest that managers are people who make things happen in their organisations, not just superior beings who perform mysterious activities on high. It also suggests that managers have to rely on the efforts of other people, conventionally called 'subordinates', who actually do the things that managers are responsible for getting done. Managers are leaders of a certain sort.

But not all leaders are managers. The trouble with the definition is that it's too wide. You'd probably agree that politicians, military officers, shop stewards are leaders but not managers in the proper sense of the word. But why not? Take someone who runs his own business. Is he a manager or a businessman — an 'entrepreneur'? And what's the difference if any? What about accountants? Don't they really control organisations by controlling their finances? What about administrators and senior professional people in public service and government ministries? What about company directors? Or for that matter a new supervisor or section leader — is he or she a manager? They all 'get things done', largely 'through other people'. Doesn't that actually make them all managers? If the simple definition isn't very helpful, let's try another approach. It is to look at the differences between the way a real manager operates and the way other people operate who do control things in organisations, but whose roles are not true management roles. Managers can get a clearer idea of what makes them managers by comparing the way they behave with the typical ways in which non-managers behave.

A. The manager v the businessman

Many people would argue there isn't much difference — they both run businesses. After a bit of thought they might concede that managers are also found in non-business organisations such as local government offices and civil service departments, places in which you'd be hard put to find many full-blooded wheeler-dealer entrepreneurs. 'So', they might say, 'that only shows a businessman is a manager who runs a profit-making company'. Well no, not exactly.

True, there are important similarities in the ways that managers and businessmen operate. Any manager worth the name does take a businesslike approach to the operation he's running. Like the businessman, he's responsible for actions and decisions that have both direct and indirect financial consequences for his organisation, whether he takes them himself or his people take them. He doesn't let himself forget it. He runs a piece of a business — or *acts* as though he does, even when his organisation actually runs on public funds. His job always has an economic purpose somewhere near the centre of it. In the use of his organisation's resources his creed is 'no waste' and 'value for money' — the value his organisation gets from his own and his people's time and efforts, the value produced by his and his people's use of physical assets such as equipment and room, materials and so on. They all represent costs to his organisation, and he sees that costs are not allowed to outrun value. The money must be used to good purpose.

The difference lies in what money really means to the manager and to the businessman. The businessman has his own money at risk. The manager doesn't — he has a professional

THE BUSINESSMAN GETS THINGS DONE PROFITABLY THROUGH BUSINESS DEALS...

responsibility for his organisation's money. This has all sorts of effects.

For the businessman, the money he makes — his profit — is a goal in itself. It decides his standard of living, even his survival, and it gives him a personal feeling of success. He wants as much of it as possible, and to get it he will take risks that for a manager would be foolhardy. His function might be defined as 'getting things done *profitably* by making business deals'.

For the manager, the money his organisation earns cannot be a personal goal. In any case, he himself is unlikely to have any real control over it unless he is at the top of his organisation (in which case he shares many of the businessman's entrepreneurial functions). He certainly *contributes* to profit. He sees that his own area of responsibility plays whatever part it can in getting revenue for his organisation — or in ensuring that revenue isn't jeopardised. He controls costs and spending in his area. But hardly any of a manager's actions are explained by calling them 'profit-motivated'.

Profit for a manager is really a yardstick, not an aim. In a commercial organisation it provides an important way for him to measure whether a thing is worth doing or not, and whether it's being done right. But he *can* manage without profit. If he's a manager in a non-profit-making organisation he's got to. *Inside* an organisation, which is where the manager is, money operates mainly as a constraint. There isn't enough of it around to do everything he might want to in pursuit of his organisation's aim, so he has to decide the priorities for allocating the resources he's been given. The aim itself depends on the organisation — to expand or hold on to a market, to provide a good and economic public service, or simply to help the organisation survive. *These* are the kinds of aim that explain why a manager does what he does.

The difference in their aims also makes the businessman and the manager use their people in different ways — if in fact the businessman *has* any people and employees. He doesn't have to. But if he does, for all that he's a risk-taker, there's one kind of risk the businessman tries to avoid — the risk of letting his employees play about with his livelihood. He keeps as many of the decisions that govern his income and his costs as he can to himself. The businessman doesn't usually delegate very well. He avoids delegating anything important if he can, and if he can't he sits on the shoulder of the unfortunate employee who gets the task. Psychologically he finds it difficult to trust others' intentions with his money and his assets.

For the manager, delegation is the name of the game — delegation not just of tasks but of whole areas of responsibility to his subordinates. The value he is after is the productivity he gets from his people's time *and* from their capabilities (the businessman often misses the point of the second).

To get that value, the manager lives on trust. The trust that's placed in him to run his operation well. The trust he places in his subordinates to get done the things he's responsible for and to use wisely the freedom he has given them to do this. But it's not blind trust — he maintains his own responsibility for these things. He chooses carefully what to delegate and to whom. He tries to ensure his subordinates are capable of coping effectively and are motivated to want to do so. He holds them accountable to him in ways that don't interfere with their personal feelings of responsibility.

Many businessmen are rather bad at doing these things — and, if the truth be known, not all that interested either. Business deals are their game, not the mechanisms that make organisations work and that draw the best from their employees.

Because of their different outlooks, businessman and manager often clash. The businessman criticises his managers for failing to take bold business initiatives and for losing sight of what it is that makes the *business* grow (as opposed to growth in the size of the organisation). The managers complain that the businessman plays his cards close to his chest, and constantly interferes with his running of the organisation. Both sides are right in one sense and wrong in another. Right in that these criticisms are often true. Wrong in that they aren't just. Each is criticising the other for not operating as he himself operates. They are criticising the different limitations in each other which actually create their different strengths.

Business organisations need the strengths of both businessman and manager. As soon as the businessman has more than about twenty or thirty employees he has an organisation that needs managing. It needs someone to take over the job of running its internal mechanisms so that the businessman can get on with what he's best at — the business deals that keep the organisation in business and make it grow. For his part the manager needs the businessman to provide him with an operation to run. No businessman, no business, no organisation eventually. However big a business organisation grows, it still needs people at the top whose strengths lie in their business acumen more than in their management abilities.

Where the businessman actually does damage is when he continues to dominate an organisation that has grown big enough to need managing. In businessman-dominated organisations you typically find crazy growed-like-Topsy organisation structures, feeble yes-men managers, lack of any real delegation of responsibility and authority — but a lot of dumping of menial tasks. There's often a lot of concealed waste about the place too. For the competent manager those organisations are jungles with hunters on the prowl. He doesn't usually stay long. Either he gets in the way of a hunter, or he finds a better-managed estate to do his farming in.

In a well-managed business organisation, businessman and manager have found a way to live together. The manager manages the estate. The businessman ranges the jungle round about to find further regions to hack out and bring into cultivation.

The crunch comes where the two meet. The businessman needs a manager with unusual qualities to work alongside him. He's got to be a manager whom the businessman can trust implicitly and is willing to take management advice from — a manager to whom the businessman *is* prepared to delegate the running of his organisation. Without such a manager the business will never develop its true potential. The manager for his part needs an understanding, a feeling for what makes the businessman tick so that he can fulfil his side of the bargain: to manage the organisation in ways that support the businessman's initiatives and maintain his trust.

B. The manager v the administrator

People in the public eye persist in talking about administrators as though they were managers: people such as government ministers, newspaper and television commentators, writers,

THE SYSTEM

academics, senior civil servants (well, they would), top businessmen (who should know better). We even have courses in 'Business Administration' which are clearly intended more for managers than for administrators. Perhaps all this is saying that people don't care what the difference is. But the manager should care. The difference is a crucial one for him. It concerns something that lies at the centre of his role but is an incidental, even an annoyance, to the administrator — the simple fact that he has subordinates to lead. Administrators may try to dispute this point. But the evidence lies in the way they actually behave in organisations, not in what they say or like to think about their behaviour. Most people who are in charge of others but who tackle their jobs as jobs of pure administration turn in some pretty appalling management performances.

The thing that most concerns the administrator is the well-oiled efficiency with which systems and procedures run. So he's a natural for the job of providing back-up for the politician. Both of them seem to agree that all you need to run anything, whether it's a government ministry or the local library in Little Piddlington, are appropriate systems based on the right policies. The administrator's world is one of all-embracing systems that depend not on people but on neat, well-ordered paperwork. In fact you can often recognise him by his talk about the 'smooth running' of his section or department, as though that were the aim of the whole exercise. You wouldn't be far wide of the mark if you described his function as 'ensuring things run *tidily* through systems.'

The trouble is that *people* generally don't behave in tidy ways. This bothers the administrator, who likes to have

12

everything neatly pigeon-holed. So he produces more and more bits of paper to define the proper ways to deal with all the 'exceptions that may arise' — meaning people who don't fit the pattern (his language gives him away). He can often become obsessed with minutiae and trivia and lose sight of why the systems are there in the first place. They become more and more complicated as the years roll by, to the point where they're vastly expensive to run and maintain. Not only that, but the staff who operate them can no longer get a clear picture of how they all hang together. When people can't do that, they can't make intelligent decisions about how and how not to apply the systems. So they have to fall back on the routine application of rules and procedures. They are used as tools rather than as live, adaptable human beings.

The manager too needs efficient systems — clear-cut and economical ways of handling things that lend themselves to routine procedures. But they aren't there just to keep things tidy. Their purpose is to allow him and his people to concentrate their attention on all the non-routine events and activities they have to deal with. To the systems he does operate, the real manager regularly applies the same tests of economy that he applies to anything else he is responsible for: 'is this system as simple and economical in its demands on people's time as it can be without making it ineffective?' He has little patience with rules and procedures that cause him or his people to spend a pound's worth of time producing a pennyworth of value. Administrators talk a lot about 'cost-effectiveness' (another popular term), but this is one of the many forms of it they constantly miss.

The central issue for the manager goes beyond efficiency. It is his operation's *effectiveness.* These aren't just words to him. To ask 'is your operation efficient'? is to question the way it does things in terms of its own internal economy. But 'is your operation effective?' questions whether the things it does really contribute to a broader purpose. A car may have a very efficient engine. But the engine's efficiency won't be much use to the owner who doesn't know how to use the gear-box.

To run his operation effectively, the manager gets his people to help with the running. Their involvement and sense of what is needed is essential if they are to play their part in contributing to its purpose. So the manager leads by ensuring that everyone is clear about the objectives and is competent to play a part. He doesn't attempt to constrict their activities in procedural straightjackets. The systems he does use tend to be fairly simple (anyway, simpler than those the administrator would devise) and aren't designed to try and cater for every eventuality. Instead he gives his people scope to use their judgement in dealing with exceptions to the rule. In other words, he delegates.

In all of this, the good manager isn't concerned solely with his people's present performance. He also tries to develop their abilities for the future by giving them experience of responsibility. To learn by experience they have to have opportunities to get into difficulties and make the odd mistake or two. He's prepared to accept these as minor setbacks if they help his people learn to become more effective in the future.

To the administrator, difficulties and mistakes are untidy — they upset the smooth running of his operation and cause him annoyance. He has an easy way to minimise them. He doesn't delegate responsibilities. He just gives his people tasks to perform.

None of this matters in organisations where administrators are managed by managers. It's the administrator-dominated organisation that's a mess — if you can see the administrator doing anything as decisive as dominating an organisation. Let's settle for saying that in some organisations he's in the ascendant. You can tell his organisation by the way most of its employees tackle their jobs, doing one thing after another in a rigid procedure-ridden way. Clock-watching is rife. Of course they have to find something to work for. But since they can't get a sense of purpose and pride in their work, the only scope for their ambition is to seek the next upgrading in status and pay — which is achieved by the time-honoured method of keeping their noses clean. Morale is never better than so-so. It drops through the floor when the organisation is going through a difficult time. However bad it gets, no one at senior level will ever be concerned enough to do anything about it.

In such organisations, management is flabby. Senior people are more worried about protecting and enhancing their own positions than ensuring their subordinates are doing a reasonable job of management. The administrator sees the staff at lower levels as bodies filling jobs, not as people. If someone is there a job is considered to be filled, however badly he does it. He won't get fired because dismissals are unpleasant and untidy, and administrators are terribly prone to look the other way when there are difficulties with people. They'll assume that the difficulties will be overcome by the foolproof nature of the systems.

In fact, since systems *can't* run everything a lot of responsibilities accidentally get dumped on people down the line. If a lower-level manager has an impossible subordinate to cope with, he's just got to make the best of it. He won't get any support from his administrator boss. If a junior member of staff makes an expensive mistake, he must have failed to use the system properly. It's never the administrator's fault that his junior staff had the *opportunity* to make such a mistake.

Not only is management flabby in administered organisations. The organisations themselves become flabby with growth far beyond the size that's really needed to perform their functions. The administrator encourages this growth because it enhances his position: the more people he has beneath him, the higher his status and grade. So his way of reckoning the number of staff he ought to have isn't the manager's way — to size up the work to be done and then calculate the people needed to do it. He looks over at other administered organisations and uses their staff numbers as a base for his own requirements. As those other organisations are themselves run by people doing the same thing, you don't need a degree in statistics to fathom out the consequences.

Yet organisations do need the administrator's abilities in setting up and running their systems. Managers often lack the patience to do this well and prefer to delegate it to a good administrator with a clear brief on what's needed. The problem is the administrator who's in a management job. There the only solution is for him to learn how to operate as a manager in coping with his management responsibilities.

C. The manager v the accountant

Accountants are seen by many managers as necessary evils inside organisations. Necessary they are, certainly. Evils they may or may not be. That might depend on how effectively they perform their special role in collaboration with managers. On the other hand, it might depend more on the managers' own effectiveness in interpreting accountancy information and advice to keep their operations running economically. Faults lie very often more on the managers' side than on the accountants'. But in playing their financial role in an organisation, accountants are not — repeat, *not* — managers. Indeed, they very often make poor managers in the one management role they do have — in running the accounts department.

This is a view that gets many accountants hot under the collar. 'Very well', they say, 'managers are there to manage the operations and the people in their departments. But we manage the money they use'. To which the answer *ought* to be 'rubbish!' If it isn't rubbish, then the managers aren't fulfilling the vital function of managing the economy of their departments.

Sadly it's often true that so-called managers abdicate their economic responsibilities to accountants. They feel lost and

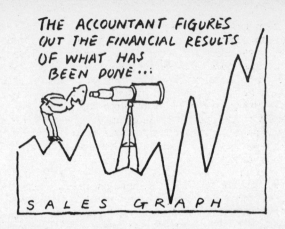

THE ACCOUNTANT FIGURES OUT THE FINANCIAL RESULTS OF WHAT HAS BEEN DONE...

SALES GRAPH

uncomfortable in discussing sheets of figures with people who so obviously know their way around the financial mysteries involved. Money isn't their business they reckon, and anyway they aren't competent to argue. So they meekly accept whatever the accountants decide. Which may do a lot for the accountants' sense of their own power, but not a lot for the good management of their organisations.

The point is that the manager *is* 'managing money' when he manages his operations and his people, whether he realises it or not. If he's a real manager he knows you can't separate them. But then, he also knows that his organisation's money isn't for the most part in the form of the stuff that chinks in a pocket or piles up in a bank vault. A lot of it can't even be figured out on sheets of paper. It's there in him, in his people, in the equipment and materials they operate with, in the space they use, in the time it takes them to do things, in the efforts they put into their jobs, in their capabilities. Money for the manager is the *value* of all these things. His job is to use that input of value to his operation to produce output of even greater value to the aims of his organisation.

The accountants' figures miss out some vital elements of all these values. 'Accountants', as Oscar Wilde might have said, 'know the price of everything and the value of nothing'.

Surprisingly (or perhaps not so surprisingly if they consider they control the whole show), accountants rarely calculate the costs they themselves create in an organisation. Even when they do, they often consider only the direct costs of their departments — their own staff and office costs. They ignore the indirect costs they cause in the wider organisation because they find them difficult to isolate and evaluate. But that doesn't remove the costs. The costs of management and staff time in satisfying the demands of complex accounting systems. The diseconomies caused by making managers regard their budgets as rigid rules for spending rather than guidelines for economy. Managers get into the habit of spending their budgets to the hilt whether the spending is worthwhile or not. They also get into the habit of using the budget as an argument for *not* taking constructive and truly economic initiatives. Accountants miss these things. Real managers know they go on and try to stop them happening.

There are a few other pretty fundamental differences between the ways that the manager and the accountant operate. One is that most of the accountant's figures look back. They are historical accounts of what has already happened in financial terms. A few important ones may try to look forward at the financial limitations on managers' actions and the possible consequences of their decisions — budgets, cash-flow forecasts, break-even analyses and that sort of thing. But the accountant is typically more at home with the certainties of the past than with the uncertainties of the future. He's happiest when he can be safely wise after the event: 'Oh but you shouldn't have done that'.

For the manager, the future is just about the only thing that really matters. He can't change the past. Its only relevance is in helping him to predict the future or to decide what to do about it. If the figures can't do that, they're of no interest to him. He steers by trying to look forward over the bows of his ship rather than by taking the accountant's stern-end seat and studying its wake.

Many accountants claim that the modern accountant has as much concern for the future as the manager has. Maybe. But there are still unconverted accountants about, and unfortunately they seem to be in the majority. The old backward-looking habits instilled over the years are just too strong for them to break.

For those accountants who do try to help managers' forward thinking, there is still a snag. They don't like risks. They prefer mapping out certainties in their financial figures, so their advice for the future is terribly cautious. They'll advise doing nothing about an opportunity that a manager would be better advised to grab. It's always safer to stand still, and it gives the accountants a feeling of security. They know they won't have to change their financial maps.

Unfortunately you don't get anywhere simply by looking at maps. Managers' jobs are to keep the organisation moving — to 'make things happen'. Accountants don't actually make anything happen for all their busy figure work, so they don't fully understand the risk that the manager must take in doing it. The risk that in trying to economise in one area, he might cause costs elsewhere that are bigger than the money saved. The risk that in trying to get his workforce to adopt more efficient methods, he might have to accept some expensive labour problems for a while. The risk that in delegating a new responsibility to a subordinate, the subordinate might make a mistake that runs up a sizeable bill. The manager will try to minimise the risks, but he can't be certain of avoiding them.

The trouble is that accountants aren't attuned to looking for these kinds of risk. They'll calculate a forecast down to the nearest penny to give themselves an illustration of safety and certainty. And there's a snag in that. A forecast that looks very exact is always a danger: because it *looks* so accurate, the manager might believe it and not look around for the risks that make nonsense of it. He has got to look for these risks himself. The accountants can't help him.

The accountants can't help the manager with something else either: to reckon what his people's abilities and pride in their work are worth to the organisation. No one expects accountants to be equipped to put a money value on these kinds of thing. But it's one thing to be unable to put a money value on something. It's entirely another thing to ignore its value. The accountants see only the cost of people, not their value. So they'll often begrudge a bit of extra spending on people that could reap far bigger rewards in raising their abilities and morale. This doesn't necessarily mean extra pay. The spending might be on training or staff meetings or better methods of selecting managers. That's the sort of spending that's first to go in an accountant-steered economy drive.

Morale and team spirit don't show up on a balance sheet. But they have a hell of an effect on how well the manager's operation runs — and therefore on its economy. Sagging morale and people at cross-purposes are very expensive items for an organisation. The manager has to judge this sort of thing when he considers his spending on his people. He can be sure the accountants won't.

This isn't a case of softies in the management ranks. It doesn't mean giving your people anything they want, to buy yourself out of labour problems. It might mean looking candidly at the rewards your people get for their efforts and fighting to make the rewards more fair — fair to those who put in the effort, and also fair to the organisation for those who *don't* put in the effort. It might mean weathering some storms from the less competent lower-paid to buy in a few people of greater ability at a higher rate. If they prove their competence and value, they'll be accepted eventually. You might even find yourself getting more respect for your tough-minded but constructive management — and there's value to the organisation in that too.

Perhaps you're limited in your scope to do such things by unions who don't believe in that particular fair pay principle, or by more senior managers who don't want their pay scales upset. That isn't your fault. But it *is* your fault if you let accountants stop you doing it.

Most of these things go straight over the head of the average accountant — which is one solid reason he isn't a manager. He doesn't see the one vital factor in managing people: they are the only resource that any organisation uses that actually can increase in value with use. If they are well managed, they'll become a greater and greater asset to the organisation as time goes on.

In organisations where the accountants have the upper hand, anything that can't be reckoned in fixed and certain financial terms is hardly reckoned at all. The vision and drive of the businessman, the development of people's abilities and spirit that is the fingerprint of the manager, both are missisng. Cautious negatives stifle positive risk-taking initiatives with the business and its people.

Accountant-dominated organisations tend to find their most real existence in the manipulations that produce balance sheets and profit-and-loss accounts. Their people and operations almost become adjuncts to the pieces of paper. The accountant-boss treats his manager-subordinates as tools to make the figures come right: 'I don't care how you do it. You've got to cut those costs'. He has a blind spot for the time needed to change something *effectively* in an organisation. His figures can be changed on the instant. He somehow assumes the same is true of operations and people. He'll mount sudden across-the-board cost-cutting drives that starve truly productive operations of the resources they need, but that still leaves waste in operations that any real manager would know should be killed outright. True economy is replaced by penny-pinching.

Despite all this, the accountant is essential in any organisation that has among its aims an economic one. Not to take over the manager's responsibility for economy, but to help him fulfil it. The accountant's role is in the first place a mechanical one — to get together all the values of things that have happened that *can* be represented in financial terms, and to arrange them so that managers can see the results of their past management translated into money. He can then help them interpret what the figures mean for their future management, spotting significant changes whose implications the managers may need to consider: 'what happened to cause that change? Should we do anything about it?' He can take the managers operational plans and turn them into budgets and cash-flow forecasts that show the managers whether their plans really make economic sense. As the plans are converted into actions he can advise the managers on the adjustments they find are needed.

If he's a good accountant he can even help managers learn the kind of financial thinking that enables them to play their proper part in all this. But he won't do this successfully unless *he* learns from the managers how to temper his financial advice with some awareness of its practical effects for their operations and people.

D. The manager v the specialist

Many management positions are filled by people whose real talent is not in 'getting something done through other people' but in doing the thing themselves. They might be members of a recognised profession or vocation — doctors, lawyers, teachers, architects, scientists . . . or they could be people who are very expert as journalists, salesmen, chefs, engineers, computor programmers and so on — occupations that many of them would call professions. Whatever they do, they are very good indeed at doing it. But each one has a narrow field. He's a specialist in his kind of work, and often has limited ability and even less interest in anything outside it.

The accountant is one kind of specialist, but he's got a special relationship with managers. You find him in any organisation in which financial management is important — as we've said, not to manage the money but to help the managers manage it. And what the accountant is doing is always relevant to the managers' work, whatever function they're managing in his organisation. That was the point we've just dealt with. Here we're looking at the professional accountant as a manager in his own department.

Specialists are often brilliant in their own line. As managers they are disastrous more often than not. The problem is created by rigid organisation structures that can't give them status and salary increases without forcing them into management roles that for them are totally inappropriate. Some specialists see the implications of this and refuse promotion above a certain level. Many realise it too late and become frustrated in a role that they know is wasting their real talents. Many more survive in

THE SPECIALIST DOES THINGS HIMSELF ...

management positions for years without ever realising what their management role is. It's not the specialists' fault. It's the fault of their superiors who appointed them to these positions.

The manager and the specialist do have a common cause. Both want to achieve high standards in whatever their operations do. But the specialist sets the standards by his own capabilities. The manager sets the standards by what his organisation needs and what his people can achieve. He also considers the economy of his operations, the morale of his people, the need to give them opportunities to develop their abilities — things that the specialist usually doesn't concern himself with too much.

The most obvious difference between the specialist's and the manager's management methods is when they're faced with some unacceptable work from their subordinates. The manager tries to use it as an opportunity to coach his subordinates if he's got the chance. The specialist takes it over himself. He concentrates on the immediate work-problems and ignores the longer-term need for his people to learn how to cope: 'I can't be bothered to explain. It's less trouble to do it myself''. In any case he finds it hard to believe they can become as competent as he is — and that is the only way they can satisfy his perfectionist standards. He delegates the smaller humdrum jobs his operation gets to do, the dogwork. The bigger or trickier tasks he keeps to himself — exactly the tasks that the manager tries to get his people involved in to give them experience.

Even with the stuff he delegates, the specialist is likely to insist that his people do it his way. He can waste hours of his own expensive time fiddling with their output to put it into the form he'd have put it in if he'd done it originally. He's nominally in charge of other people, but he still sees the core of his job as 'doing things' not 'getting things done through others'.

The manager accepts a vaiety of ways of getting something done. He doesn't insist his is the only way. He tries to help his subordinates to work out their own best way of doing it and is even willing to learn new angles from them. The Not-Invented-Here factor that bedevils so many specialists is completely absent from his approach. As long as the result is acceptable and no rules have been broken on the way he is prepared to accept it.

The biggest problems are those of the specialist who has reached a position where some of the operations he's in charge of are outside his specialist field. He feels uncomfortable with the responsibility for things he can't do himself — or can't do better than his people. His inclination is to ignore these things rather than try to learn about them. He retreats into his specialist corner that has made him feel secure and successful in life and devotes his attention to that possibly minor part of his job. And that's why he stays a specialist.

The manager is by inclination a *generalist.* He's interested in learning about anything that could be relevant to his management of his operation. His strength as a manager lies in knowing about a range of different things and in combining different kinds of ability. The higher he goes in his organisation, the wider the range of general abilities he needs. He can't become a DIY expert in everything he's responsible for. But he *can* learn enough to manage it — to know what's involved in doing it, to judge how well it's being done, to help his subordinates develop *their* expertise.

For the organisation that is run by a specialist, there is one thing that can ease his problems. Typically it's a small organisation — a professional partnership or a specialist function inside a larger organisation. That's usually enough to prevent the specialist's difficulties in managing things from becoming out of hand unless he's a rank bad boss. The true specialist isn't normally very interested in organisational growth. Morale can be quite high among his employees because they are proud to be members of his tiny crew and may have a lot of freedom in doing the things he is not interested in. He doesn't have his organisation under control, but their commitment makes up for that. As long as he's not stupid enough to recruit really poor people, his ship sails along quite happily.

It's when the specialist becomes the head of something bigger in his professional field that problems emerge. He is not usually a good picker of management talent. If he's given managers, he's often more critical of their weaknesses in his specialist field than appreciative of the value of their abilities to his organisation. And his persistent meddling with the work the lower ranks do on his hobby can make it difficult for his managers to manage. He doesn't intend any harm. He is simply trying to ensure that whatever leaves his organisation comes up to his standards. If the disciplines of working in organised ways with other people get in the way of that, the disciplines come off second best.

This isn't to criticise the specialist as a professional. It simply says he isn't a manager. An organisation needs its professionals to do specialised jobs inside it and to maintain its reputation in the world outside. If the high-ranking specialist can be relieved of the responsibilities that cause him to waste his time and his organisation's resources doing an incompetent management job, he can provide inside the organisation a model of excellence for others in his function to aspire to. What he needs is a manager working alongside him to manage the department that he himself is nominally in charge of — perhaps a deputy or an assistant. The title doesn't matter. What does matter is the manager's function: the specialist leaves the management to the manager.

E. The manager v the shop steward

Many a tough and effective shop steward has turned into an equally tough and effective manager. So where's the difference here? Perhaps little in those organisations whose senior 'managers' treat their shop stewards as another arm of management, informing them of managements' intentions before (or without) informing their own supervisors, involving them in negotiations to which lower-level managers are not party, looking to them to arrange work-force rosters and to maintain the discipline of their union members. But this effectively pulls the management rug from under the feet of all those other managers. It destroys their will to manage and their capacity to command the respect of their people.

The difference between managers and shop stewards is in the order of priority they give to their aims — what it is they are trying to 'get done'. Both have (or ought to have) a concern for their people's welfare and for their best interests. Both need to understand their people as individuals and as groups. Both are in a sense engaged in a competition for leadership. But for the manager, all of these are means to an end. When the chips are down the manager is there to serve his organisation's interests.

For the shop steward, his members' interests are an end in themselves. He is there to serve those interests (and possibly his

THE SHOP-STEWARD PROTECTS THE INTERESTS OF HIS MEMBERS...

union's, but that's another story). His function might be defined as 'to get things done *for* other people' — his members.

It's true that many a shop steward sees the success of the organisation that employs him and his members as important, and will privately give constructive advice on shop floor matters to managers that he can trust. But in his role, helping the organisation's efficiency and productivity is an intelligent way to enhance his members' welfare and financial security. He has no particular responsibility for the organisation itself, nor should managers expect him to have it. They are paid to manage. He isn't.

In any case, the shop steward reaches and holds his position in an entirely different way from the manager. He is elected and re-elected annually by his members: the manager is appointed by more senior managers in his organisation, for an undefined period usually. The shop steward's followers can reject him when they choose and replace him with another leader more to their liking. The manager's subordinates have no such power — in some cases the more's the pity. However ineffective he may be as a leader, he can't be deposed by those beneath him and is usually unlikely to get fired by those above him who were responsible for his appointment. For the good manager, this gives him the security to take unpopular but necessary decisions. That usually isn't possible for the shop steward. He may see clearly enough the direction in which the long-term interests of his members lie, but often he cannot be seen to move in that direction without jeopardising his position with them.

All of this might suggest that shop stewards are simply

misplaced managers. Perhaps many are. But the differences between the shop steward's and the manager's situations and their aims makes a sizeable difference to the abilities actually needed in the two jobs. In the first place, shop stewards don't have to develop habits of thinking in terms of economy. They may spot diseconomies in the organisation and use them to support their case for the ability of the organisation to fork out for their members: wasted materials, overpaid staff in departments other than those their members are in, expensive management-created muddles whose costs the organisation seems to have been able to swallow without a blink. They may even try pot-shots at management perks. But this doesn't mean they can *run* things economically, which is one of a manager's main functions.

In the second place, shop stewards don't have to develop the balance the manager tries to keep in caring for his people *and* his organisation. A lot of them do — but they don't *have* to. The anti-management militants among shop stewards may be a minority, but they demonstrate the point. In fact many union members would consider a sense of balance in their shop steward a positive disadvantage for union–management negotiations. The manager has to weigh one thing against another in almost every major decision he takes: the quantity and quality of work against the time available to do it; the demands of the moment against longer-term needs; his concern for his people against his concern for his organisation. His job is a constant struggle to keep a proper balance between conflicting requirements.

In the union-dominated organisation all this balance and economy goes by the board. Almost every management decision of any consequence to the internal working of the organisation is fixed by what the militant shop steward will wear and what he won't — which might depend on the militancy of his members or on his own appetite for power. Managers themselves don't try to explain to their people the consequences of these decisions for the organisation, and lack the negotiating skills or determination to counter the shop steward's crude threats or subtle machinations. So the organisation's case goes by default. Demands are framed on the basis of 'class warfare' or whatever other philosophy the union members subscribe to, and voices of reason are shouted down in union meetings. In the worst cases, managers are forbidden to call meetings of their own people among the union members, even meetings to discuss operational matters, for fear they might undermine the steward's own influence. They are encouraged *not* to have a proper sense of responsibility for their people.

The organisation loses. But so do the union members. Featherbedded jobs, lax discipline and lack of positive management don't actually make people happier or do anything for their morale. If it's a business organisation, they don't do anything for the prospects of the organisation or of the employment it provides either. Even organisations run for the benefit of their employees need managers, as workers' cooperatives have discovered.

In a managed organisation the manager maintains his authority to manage. But he knows that much of his authority stems from the willingness of his people — the shop steward's members — to follow his lead and to convert his instructions into effective action. He needs their respect and trust no less than the shop steward does. The shop-steward-turned-manager often starts with a big advantage in his understanding of the things that build or destroy that respect and trust. For him the question is how well he can learn to make balanced judgements and decisions and to grapple with his new responsibility for economy.

F. The manager v the politician

Managers and politicians are involved together in many organisations. The results are usually frustrating for the managers and often damaging to the organisations. Whether they are real ones or the players of 'organisational politics', politicians are a bloody nuisance inside organisations.

The elected variety must take a lot of the blame for the gross diseconomies of the average local government department. Not so much the externally visible waste of blocks of flats pulled down within a few years of being put up or palatial council offices constructed at vast expense. The real damage is in the hidden internal waste that goes on because of the councillors' ignorance of the requirements for effective management in their organisations. They score top of the league of those who waste resources through their persistent habit of appointing non-managers to management positions in their organisations. The player variety at large in our corporations and industrial giants work in the guts of an organisation and have an even more insidious effect on its health. They are potent sources of demoralisation, but the inefficiences they cause hardly ever surface into public awareness of what's going on.

Elected politicians can, at least, claim to be essential to a democracy. Many of their decisions and actions are based on public concerns that over-ride the economic priorities of a

POLITICIANS MAKE REGULATIONS TO PREVENT PEOPLE FROM DOING THINGS AGAINST THE PUBLIC INTEREST..

manager. Even when the outcome isn't totally to the public's benefit, the intentions are usually good: 'should we keep that uneconomic school open for the sake of the community?' 'Should we maintain that uneconomic bus service for the sake of the few people who otherwise would be isolated?' When managers consider such questions, they tend to calculate the value of the publicity their organisations will get for their public-spirited behaviour. There is nothing wrong in that — they are simply performing their proper function as managers. True, some politicians seem to look more for favourable publicity for themselves among the voters than for actions and initiatives which are truly in the public's interest. which is only to say that politicians can be as self-serving as anyone else, but that is not their public function.

The point is the different priority that politicians and managers give to money. Early on in most decisions he takes, the manager calculates money values. He asks 'is it worth spending £X to get £Y value?' and 'how certain is it that we'll get £Y value?' and 'could we spend only half £X and still get threequarters of £Y value — and will that be enough for our purpose?' In *his* decisions, the politician thinks first of his political goals. Money values tend to take a back seat in his mind. He will often ignore the true costs of the initiatives he has helped get under way until the money has been committed and it's going to be either too politically damaging or too hideously — and publicly — wasteful to backtrack.

The common ground for politicians and managers is an interest in influencing the course of events. But their purpose in wielding influence and their methods of doing it are worlds apart.

27

The politician does it by getting laws made and systems established that act as curbs on what he regards as anti-social behaviour in society at large. This isn't his only method, but it is his main method of wielding influence. Whether his intention is to make society 'more fair' or 'more free', much of his effort is directed towards trying to prevent people from getting unfair advantages or from restricting others' freedom of choice. His function might be defined as 'getting things done to some people for other people's benefit'. Who the 'some people' and 'other people' are will depend largely on his political creed. Broadly speaking, the politician's approach is 'find out what little Tommy is up to and stop him'. And what stops little Tommy isn't the personal intervention of the politician himself but the regulatory systems he has helped establish. Politicians have a marvellous faith in the power of systems to run things — including the organisations they are nominally in charge of.

The manager's influence on events is much more direct. He actually does make things happen in the bit of society he manages. Not that he spends his time running around giving orders. For most of the time his people know what they have to get on with and don't need him to come charging in to spur their efforts. But a lot of his activity is directed to adjusting the ways they get on with things so that the final result is better or obtained more economically. And he does this through his personal intervention. The manager is constantly *there*. He knows that managers like him, not systems, run organisations and that the systems are only as good as the people who operate them.

The differences in influence are vast, but so are the differences between the methods by which the politicians and the manager wield their influence. Both realise they lead to a certain extent by the consent of those led — the electorate for the politician, his subordinates for the manager. But the politician's career depends on his ability to win elections, and that means he needs to court public popularity. He has to look good to the voters. This puts pressure on him to 'lead from behind' — to watch the way that public opinion is drifting so that he can match his words and actions to whatever the public seem to want at the time. As the saying goes 'a week is a long time in politics', and most politicians know the dangers of nailing your flag to a flagpole that may quickly turn into your gibbet. So the politician gets used to working within short time spans, avoiding upsetting too many people or being proved wrong. He can sometimes seem more concerned not to look foolish than to uncover and correct mistakes.

The problems begin when the politician applies these

habitual methods of working to his control of his organisation. He appoints administrators rather than managers to the key positions in his organisation because administrators tend not to argue about the organisational diseconomies his policies and decisions cause. Even when they see the waste, they'll quietly cover it up rather than make an unpleasant noise about it. Managers would home in on it and try to do something about it in ways the politician would call 'undemocratic' — although it's unlikely that an organisation can be democratic in the politician's sense and still be economic and effective.

Administrators won't bother him with questions about long-term aims either. They'll cover up the discontent in their organisations caused by short-term mind-changing and lack of information about intentions for the future. Managers would push him to establish long-term policies on which they could plan their operations economically and keep their people in the picture. So, for many reasons, the politician prefers not to have managers around the place.

For a manager, short-term decisions are often immensely wasteful. In getting things done he needs some assurance that what's done today doesn't back up into some expensive consequences tomorrow — or next month, next year, in five years' time. Many of the things he's responsible for keeping moving or getting under way can't be reversed at a moment's notice without causing costly chaos or even costlier sapping of his people's commitment. He has to have some basis on which to plan the future for his own part of the organisation. And his leadership doesn't depend on his popularity among his people — their respect for sure, but that doesn't mean avoiding things they might not like. He cannot let himself get into a situation where he feels constrained to avoid taking action on breaches of discipline or to duck necessary decisions that his subordinates (or anyone else) may not be too happy about.

The politician has another organisational disability. He does most of his active work of influencing the course of events in committees. He operates a kind of group responsibility, whether on a principle of many-heads-are-better-than-one or through unwillingness to take a personal responsibility for his decisions ('Well, it was a committee decision you know'). This might or might not be reasonable for political decisions, but it certainly isn't a sensible way to take organisational decisions.

Managers don't operate in committees because they have a different concept of responsibility. They attend them certainly, listen, take part, even run them — but they don't let committee decisions get in the way of their personal responsibilities. Every real manager feels *personally* responsible for whatever happens in his own defined area of his organisation's operations. He accepts that responsibility and expects to have an equally personal authority given to him to decide whatever has to be decided to fulfil it. He knows that he cannot blame a committee for any badly-judged decision on something to do with his neck of the woods. If the decision was wrong, *he* should have known it and got it changed.

This doesn't mean to say that the manager ignores others' opinions about what should or should not have been done. He interprets democracy in his organisation as taking account of the views of other people who have knowledge of what's involved or interests in the outcome of whatever he's deciding. But when he does make up his mind it's his own mind. He'll listen to his own people and to his colleagues and seniors, he'll observe what's going on in and around his patch and he'll base his decisions on that knowledge. He won't operate blind or deaf.

But neither will he allow others to interfere with decisions about his operation that he knows *he* should be taking, or to meddle with things that are *his* responsibility. The selection of people who'll be his subordinates is for him a key decision and he'll want to have a hand on that handle, at the very least a right of veto. And his people will look to him for leadership, not to a committee.

The contrasts between the politician and the manager come to a head over this question of selecting people to fill vacancies. The manager runs personal interviews based on a clear idea of what abilities the job needs. If it's a management job, he wants the best information he can get during each interview on how well the candidate can operate as a manager in the job. Councillors prefer to operate in selection panels (the committee again) to interview candidates for management posts in their authority. Without any clear idea of the management abilities needed in a post, each panel member puts questions to the candidates. His questions are chosen as much to impress his colleagues on the panel with his own wisdom or perception as to get useful information from the candidates. And the selection is more often on the basis of how well each candidate impresses the panel as an interviewee than on his likely effectiveness in the job. More weight is given to his views than to any evidence he might let slip about his management ability or inability. Faced with the need to select a horse, the panel chooses a camel.

But when all is said and done, the worst sappers of an organisation's effectiveness and morale are the other kind of politicians — those who play organisational politics. Their role has none of the virtues of the elected politician's function, but all his disabilities and then some. Their claims that this or that issue is 'political' is usually a hint that someone's reputation is at stake or that a decision will be based on personal interests, not those of the organisation and its people. To ensure that their own interests will be among those served, they spend a lot of their time manipulating information at committee tables or in the offices of more senior people. They are secretive over past errors or future intentions to save trouble for themselves or for those whose favours they are courting. Their constant concern is 'who is right', never 'what is right', and they are experienced enough in calculating political winners and losers during battles at more senior levels to ensure they are on the winner's side when the smoke has cleared.

They wield power by keeping others in the dark or by making them anxious with snippets of information. That this harms the organisation by destroying the trust that's needed between managers and their people is of no concern to them. Their staff hardly see them. But any reasonably adept organisational politician knows how to fend off the responsibility for his management failures. He can do it with a barrage of over-explanation — or in the last resort by attacking the incompetence or ill-will of colleagues and subordinates.

Anything less like management behaviour would be hard to imagine. The incredible thing is that all these antics are so widely accepted among managers inside our organisations. Accept them, and you accept that integrity is of no consequence in management.

G. The manager v the military

The differences between the role of managers and the roles of officers and NCOs in the armed forces are so obvious that most people overlook their similarities. Yet for anyone who can compare the experiences of being led by good officers during military service and by good managers in civvy street, the similarities are more striking than the differences. Their aims may be different, but they have a lot of common ground in their priorities.

Both manager and officer exist to 'get things done through other people'. Their purpose in life is human activity, making things happen, and the things they make happen are not so vastly different from each other even if their consequences are. Anyway, there are huge differences between the activities run by different managers in different organisations. Take for instance the difference between managing the deafening union-dominated room where the big presses roll at night in a Fleet

THE MILITARY OFFICER GETS THINGS DONE FOR MILITARY ENDS BY OTHER PEOPLE...

PLAN

Street newspaper, pressures mounting as deadlines approach, and managing a long-term research project with a small team of dedicated people in a quiet corner of Hertfordshire. There's a bigger difference there than there is between many a manager's operations and a military officer's.

There is, it's true, an essential difference between the circumstances the manager and the officer operate in. The manager is usually working in an organisation that exists to serve society's daily wants and needs and that is itself a part of normal society (unless he's working at Harwell or Aldermaston). The officer works in an organisation that exists to cope with what society doesn't want — dangerous crises — and in an organisation that's largely cut off from society, especially when it performs that function. Wars in the street are not yet a common feature of life for most of us.

The difference in circumstances creates obvious differences between the codes of discipline that the manager and the officer work within. Discipline is important for both of them, but there's a pretty wide gap between what they mean by it. Organisations that exist to cope with society's crises typically operate a fairly rigid disciplinary code. This applies to fire brigades and police forces as well as to the military. In a crisis, people have to respond fast to the orders they're given if they're to deal effectively with swift-moving, uncertain and dangerous situations, and often enough for the sake of their own lives. With the enemy coming over the top of the hill the officer can't call a meeting to decide what to do, or expect his soldiers to work out their own ways of dealing with the emergency. Their habits and disciplined obedience to orders are vital when they're in action — habits that have been instilled into them through the disciplines of drill parades and salutes.

Organisations that are managed rather than officered don't need this kind of discipline. Discipline yes, but not military-style discipline. It would even be damaging to their effectiveness. Managers and their people operate in situations that move more slowly than the situations on the battlefield. But the situations are often quite subtle and complex in the range of things that have to be considered. They're also generally more normal and predictable. Through experience the manager's people become familiar with the ways the situations can be expected to develop, and can use this knowledge to estimate what's likely to happen next. So the subordinates can often see as well as the manager can, sometimes better, how to deal with problems. They can use their own initiative without causing chaos for the rest of the organisation. As long as they are clear about their responsibilities, the manager doesn't have to be there all the time to give them orders. He can use part of his time for his other management concerns.

So the manager works by delegating responsibilities rather than by continual order-giving. Right down to the lowest level in the organisation, managers are involved in trying to get their people to feel a sense of personal obligation for a piece of the action. The more responsibility their people can cope with, the more time the managers at each level have for making things happen in the bigger, longer-term aspects of their *own* responsibilities — planning, organising, anticipating problems, developing their people. Rigid disciplines would not encourage their people to think things out for themselves and would make them too dependent on orders from above.

Military-style discipline would have another snag for the effectiveness of the manager's organisation too. It would repel many of the people the organisation needs in its employment. The specialists, the accountants, the administrators, the managers, even the work-force that the organisation needs on its payroll aren't exactly the sort of people who expect to be subjected to that kind of discipline. The more able they are, the more scope they have to choose their employer rather than the other way around. So the disciplines of the managed organisations are no stricter than they need to be to maintain people's morale and their effectiveness in working together.

However rigid or relaxed it is, discipline has occasionally to be enforced on rule-breakers. Here again the military do things differently from the manager. Even though they don't put soldiers in front of firing squads any longer, they can make the consequences of defiance of authority or wilful negligence pretty uncomfortable with confinements to camp, guard-room detentions and arduous or humiliating 'extra duties'. Many managers feel, perhaps regretfully, that their own sanctions are far more limited. It would be more accurate to say they're different. Most organisations have disciplinary procedures which create perfectly effective sanctions against those who persistently flout their disciplines, including dismissal if the offence is grave enough. It's up to the managers to use them properly — which doesn't mean running to the disciplinary procedures for every minor infringement any more than it means ignoring rank bad discipline.

In any case, the officer doesn't maintain good discipline among his troops by the threat of disciplinary action. Nor does the manager among his staff. His own leadership and the support he gets for it from his superiors, the morale and commitment that stems from this, the firmness and fairness of the ways he operates the rules — these things count for more in maintaining discipline than wielding sticks big or little. If discipline is poor in his operation or he's having to keep it by forever playing the heavy-handed schoolmaster, there's something wrong with his management, not with his men. The military think so too: 'there are no bad units, only bad officers'. Good leadership is a priority for both manager and officer, and this makes them cousins under the skin.

The one really crucial difference between the manager's role and the officer's is the end result of their efforts. The manager is there to get an economic result. The officer is there to get a military result — on the final analysis, to win battles. (Many a manager working in an organisation cursed with militant unionism might not be too sure even of this difference, but his battles are for the right to command his own people. That's not the same thing).

The result of this difference in aim is to give manager and officer very different attitudes to economy. The military are not financially orientated. In fact it's important for them *not* to be, otherwise they'd be busy looking at financial statements when they should be working out military tactics. In wars (which is when the military really come into their own), budgets are open-ended: 'do it whatever the financial cost'.

The values that officers calculate aren't expressed in money but in human life. They economise in the loss of their own men and equipment to maintain their forces' morale and fighting strength for the next battle. It's for the politicians and the civil servants to count the financial cost to the nation.

Managers *must* think in financial terms. The economic angle in their function means money values one way or another. Even when the values can't be pinned down in a profit and loss statement, they're still there having an effect on their organisations' financial economy. So the manager, in almost every decision he makes, has to weigh up the financial consequences for his organisation. He has developed *habits* of trying to run things economically.

This is the main problem for the ex-officer who has moved into a management job. He may find it difficult to get accustomed to the politics of civvy-street organisations, or to accept their frequent inefficiency and lack of care for their people. But these things offend the manager too. The thing that makes the essential difference between them is the manager's ingrained habit of seeing costs in everything and assessing the costs against the pay-off. It takes a long time for most ex-officers to acquire that habit and to pick up the kind of financial understanding that goes along with it.

Let's square one thing away before we drop all these management comparisons. We've been looking at people who *normally* don't play a management role in an organisation, however useful or necessary a role they may have. (You could argue that in that case managers themselves often don't play a management role either. We'll come back to that problem a bit later).

This doesn't mean it's impossible for people in these other roles to act as managers. Some businessmen make a very good fist of managing their organisations themselves. They get their firms well-organised, they delegate to their people, they keep morale high, they run the outfit with an eye to economy — and show all the signs that a manager is at work. What they're like as businessmen we're not qualified to say, but their firms' profit and growth records often look pretty healthy. The same goes for the other 'non-management' types — administrators, accountants, specialists and the rest. They *can* all learn to combine their own particular skills with managerial abilities if their jobs include management responsibilities along with their other functions. The fact that most of them don't do this doesn't mean it can't be done.

Some of them employ managers — businessmen and politicians particularly. So it's not unreasonable to expect them to have an idea of what management is, as opposed to their own function, and what kind of a job they should expect their manager employees to do. Others are more often employed by managers — accountants, administrators, specialists of various kinds, shop stewards even (as members of a manager's work-force of course, hardly in their shop steward function). So it makes sense for them to understand the way their boss is trying to operate if he's a genuine manager. The manager himself gets a clearer idea of where *he* stands among all those other people if he understands how their roles and approaches are likely to differ from his own.

Managers work in economically-based organisations — that's basic to their job. No such organisations, no managers. And their organisations exist to do things in society: things for their customers, for their employees, for their shareholders or ratepayers (which ever they have), and for society itself — the public. The manager's job is to try to help his organisation play fair with all these interested parties without squandering in the process that essential resource, money. His job may at times be very complicated, but it has a basis that can be defined quite simply:

> 'The manager gets things done *economically* through other people'.

What management isn't

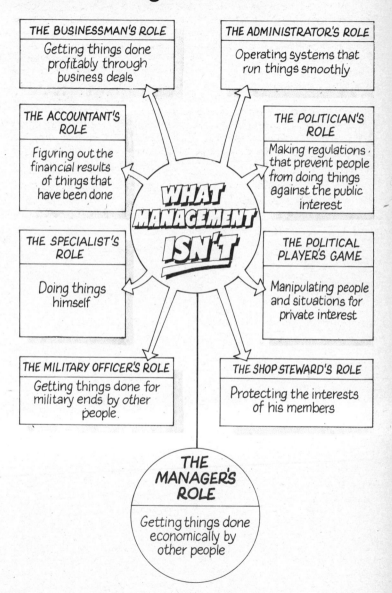

THE BUSINESSMAN'S ROLE
Getting things done profitably through business deals

THE ADMINISTRATOR'S ROLE
Operating systems that run things smoothly

THE ACCOUNTANT'S ROLE
Figuring out the financial results of things that have been done

THE POLITICIAN'S ROLE
Making regulations that prevent people from doing things against the public interest

THE SPECIALIST'S ROLE
Doing things himself

THE POLITICAL PLAYER'S GAME
Manipulating people and situations for private interest

WHAT MANAGEMENT ISN'T

THE MILITARY OFFICER'S ROLE
Getting things done for military ends by other people.

THE SHOP STEWARD'S ROLE
Protecting the interests of his members

THE MANAGER'S ROLE
Getting things done economically by other people

3. The need for management

If you're called a supervisor, you're in a management job — you're responsible for getting things done economically through the efforts of your people. And so are a lot of other people in jobs that don't actually carry the label 'manager'. An overseer or a foreman on a building site is in a management job. A scientist leading a small research team in a laboratory is in a management job. So is someone in charge of a group of clerks in a local government office, or someone who heads up a function in a hotel — a chief receptionist or head waiter. Even though they're near the bottom of an organisation chart, they're all in jobs that require some management ability to do them properly. Whether or not each of them is tackling his or her job *like* a manager may be another question entirely.

The same applies at the top of the organisation chart. Company directors are usually managers when they can get time off from being businessmen. If they're executive directors they each head up all the people in a function of their organisation, so their jobs too require a management approach. Chief officers in local government *ought* to be managers if only they could stop devoting all their time to being administrators or politicians' aides. Executives *might* be managers, but that depends on whether they've got any subordinates. Some of them haven't. Now and again you can find someone who's called a manager but who's in a department of one — himself. For all that he's got the title, he's not a manager because his job lacks one of the essential qualifications. He has no people to lead. Managers are people who are employed in management jobs, whatever the labels might or might not be.

Their jobs come in all shapes and sizes. Some are done in overalls, some in city suits. Some need high-powered brains, some need only basic commonsense. More often than not, one job is so different from another that the managers in them couldn't swap places. Frequently they couldn't even begin to understand what's involved in each others' jobs. There's such a vast range of things managers do and kinds of knowledge and experience they need to do them that any one manager's job can usually be done only by another manager with very similar knowledge and experience. So can anyone talk of a manager's ability to manage his operation as something that *all* managers share?

Well, if that *is* a question it misses the point. Try comparing managers with musicians. The violinist and the clarinettist each plays an instrument that requires a different set of skills and techniques. They couldn't swap instruments. And if one is a classical musician and the other a jazz artist, they're probably limited in their abilities to play each others' music. But if they're real musicians, they both share a general musical ability. If one has the technique to play his instrument but lacks musicianship, the other can tell. He doesn't have to play the instrument himself to know that.

It's the same for managers. Like the clarinettist and the violinist, the managers in a factory and a sales force are physically doing very different things because the work they are managing is so different. Like the members of a symphony orchestra and a jazz band, the managers of a bank and a construction company operate in very different ways because their organisations are in different fields. Sure, they all 'plan' and 'control' their operations, but none of them can do those things for the others' operations. They can't change places. But if they're managers, their *approach* to what they're doing will be remarkably similar. It's the approach that any real manager takes to the management part of his job. The point of this chapter is to pin down exactly what the similarities are.

We have to start with the things that create a need for managers — the organisations they work in. The basic features of organisations create the basic features needed in their management, and although organisations themselves can be very different and their operations can be worlds apart they do all share some common features.

The managed organisation

Any organisation that's managed exists to DO CERTAIN THINGS in society, and the things it does are governed by its PURPOSE. They're not done just for the sake of doing them or because someone in the organisation feels that this or that activity would be nice to have aboard — or at least they *oughtn't* to be done for these reasons. Everything that's done should contribute in some useful way to what the organisation is there *for*. If it doesn't contribute, it gets in the way of the activities that do contribute. The purpose might be to supply a *market* with a certain range of goods or services — in which case the organisation was set up originally by a businessman. Or its purpose might be to do certain things for the public generally or to regulate the public's behaviour in certain ways — in which case the organisation was originally created by politicians.

To do these things, the organisation needs RESOURCES. It needs land and buildings and equipment and materials — all the 'physical assets' of the organisation. It also needs services like electricity, water, telephones and so on. But two resources are basic. The organisation couldn't begin to operate without them.

One is the MONEY put into it. The businessman funds his organisation by putting his own money into it and by persuading shareholders to invest in it and banks to lend money to it. The politicians fund *their* organisations by forcing the general public and business organisations to pay taxes and rates. However it gets its money, the organisation has a duty to the people who've put the money in to see that it is used in the best way possible to satisfy the purpose and that the resources bought with it aren't wasted by inefficiency or extravagance. If the organisation can achieve its aims with less money, it's got a duty to do that too. The money is basic because it buys all the other resources that the organisation needs.

The other basic resource is the organisation's PEOPLE — its employees. They're basic because the organisation 'does things' only in the sense that its people do things. The money pays for them too of course, but their value as a resource doesn't depend simply on how much they're paid. It also depends on how competent they are to do the things the organisation needs done, on how clearly they understand what they've got to do, on how willing they are to put their best effort into doing these things, on how effectively they work together. And all *these* things are decided by two questions that are absolutely fundamental to the effectiveness of any organisation.

The first is the question of how well its people are *organised*. The main point of organising people is to COORDINATE what each person does with what everyone else is doing. This can't be done if they're all working as a mass in a hugh human ant-hill. So the organisation groups them by the different kinds of work they do. It puts together in each group people whose work is similar or closely connected. Then rather than individuals having to try to coordinate what they're doing with what everyone else is doing, the groups can be coordinated — which is slightly easier.

But there are ways and ways of organising people and some organisations don't do it very well. They get groups working at cross purposes wasting each others' time and resources and generally preventing people from using their abilities fully to get the right things done. Finding a good way of organising the groups isn't easy, and it should be something that managers occasionally devote a bit of time to thinking about.

The second fundamental question is the way the groups are *led*. The main point of leadership is to maintain people's MORALE and their SENSE OF PURPOSE. Any group of people needs leadership. It's a very basic human need. And in itself it isn't a very complicated or time-consuming kind of role — demanding, yes, but difficult, no. More than anything else, it's to do with the leader's character, his attitude to the others in his group and how clear he is about what they're all trying to do together.

With the wealth of human talent available in most organisations, it shouldn't be difficult to find enough people who've got those qualities. They exist all right. They're there in each organisation. But organisations are remarkably bad at picking them out and in showing them how their talents should be used. In most organisations that are managed, there are management positions occupied by people who won't — or can't — operate as leaders, who don't even think of themselves as leaders. But far more are filled by intelligent people who perceive the need but get no guidance or encouragement in meeting it. Leadership is a lost art in modern organisations.

It's true that managers have more than a leadership role. They also have to cope with all the complications of trying to coordinate the different kinds of work going on in their organisations and of finding economical ways of doing it. In a big organisation that has managers working at many different levels, the problems of coordinating everything to achieve the aims and of avoiding waste of effort and resources become highly involved. The higher a manager is in the organisation, the more far-reaching are the problems he has to tackle. If he doesn't tackle them successfully, his part of the organisation cannot be fully effective. That reduces the effectiveness of the whole organisation because organisations don't work in bits and pieces — an effective bit here, an ineffective piece there. Until there's a take-over bid or the official receiver moves in, the thing either works properly as a whole or it doesn't. If an important bit is weak, the whole organisation suffers.

From your standpoint in the organisation it is easy to under-rate these difficulties in the jobs of managers at more senior levels. Perhaps you should ask yourself whether you make enough effort to try to understand. But then — you have a busy job, sorting out the problems of getting things done in your section and maintaining your leadership of your people. And perhaps those senior managers don't make much effort to keep you in the picture either. All the same, if a lot of your hard-working activity isn't to be wasted, you need to understand the kinds of problems that have to be tackled at more senior levels and the kinds of contribution you can make to what the managers above you are trying to do. It's partly up to you to be prepared to find out, and it's partly up to your superiors to stop being so secretive with all that 'confidential' management information. Most of it is only confidential for 'political' reasons in any case. And this applies just as much to you as a boss if that is what you are.

The point is that all the managers in an organisation have to work together if the organisation itself is to work properly, and that includes everyone from supervisor right up to chief executive. There are no 'commissioned' and 'non-commissioned' ranks in management. They're all managers performing that leadership-plus-coordination-plus-economy-seeking job that is called Management.

The need for management

4. The manager's job

A lot of the confusion about management stems from a failure to understand one basic feature of every manager's job: *it isn't all 'management'*. Obviously some of it must be management, otherwise the person doing it wouldn't qualify for the label 'Manager'. But many managers are so proud of their managerial status that they try to insist that everything they do is 'management' — which explains at least half of the muddled thinking that goes on about what 'managing' really means. The first thing is to distinguish clearly between the management and non-management parts of the manager's job.

A. The non-management part

Every manager in an organisation takes on a part of the responsibility for keeping the organisation working properly. His

45

job is to get things done economically by the people on his patch — the part of the organisation he's been given to manage. That's the management part of his job.

But that isn't all. Besides getting his people to do things, the manager does some of the things himself. A sales manager might call on a customer; a clerical supervisor might lend a hand with the clerical work; an engineering superintendent might repair a machine fault. Nearly every manager's job includes some non-management work like this — a sort of managerial Do-It-Yourself.

Some DIY the manager may do to help with the workload or because he happens to be on the spot. Some may be specialist work that no one else can do. Some he may feel is too difficult or too 'responsible' to leave to his subordinates. Some may frankly be nothing more than interference with things they're doing — either because they're having difficulties or because he's not satisfied with their efforts. Whatever the reason for doing it, the important point to recognise is that when a manager does it *he isn't 'managing'*.

If the organisation is going to work effectively and not waste the money it pays its managers to manage, they have to find a fair way of dividing their time between their management activities and DIY work. Some managers who are obsessed with the status of their position refuse to do any DIY at all because they reckon they're above that sort of thing. (We're not talking here about managers who are prevented from doing DIY by silly demarcations.) That's not a real manager's argument. He'll chop wood and fetch water if it helps. But he doesn't fall into the other hole — the hole the manager is in who spends too much time on DIY. Why is he in that hole? Probably because he feels more comfortable down there! The trap is that he often enjoys doing DIY. It's usually easier for him than his management work, and he might feel it's a way for him to 'show the lads there's *something* I can do round here'. The real manager takes on some of the DIY but on two conditions: it mustn't divert him from managing properly, and it mustn't remove interest and responsibility from his subordinates' jobs.

How *should* managers split their time? That all depends. Usually the main thing that decides it is a manager's level in his organisation. As a general rule the higher his level, the more time he needs to spend on management and the less time he has for DIY.

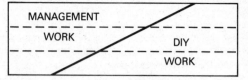

Time available

Top-level manager

MANAGEMENT

Middle-level manager

WORK

DIY

Lower-level manager

WORK

At the lower level, the supervisors and section leaders and foremen may actually be able to spend more time on DIY than on management — without neglecting their management responsibilities. This doesn't mean their management role is easy or unimportant. It's vitally important, though very often under-rated by status-conscious people at higher levels.

As the manager who is *directly* in charge of the workforce, the supervisor is managing the people who actually do whatever the organisation exists to do. Often he has more people to lead than any of the managers further up the line, so his leadership ability is as important to the organisation as anyone else's. But he shouldn't have the really complicated problems of coordination and economy to worry about if his superiors are doing *their* management jobs properly.

At the middle level, the department heads and unit managers have bigger and more difficult management questions and problems to tackle. So if they spend too much time on DIY, they *will* be neglecting their management responsibilities. Remember that DIY for them doesn't only mean operational work. It also includes getting involved in doing the management work of their supervisors and section heads. That too counts as DIY for the middle-level manager.

At the top level are directors, chief officers, general managers who've got a whole organisation to manage. So they've little time available for DIY (which for them of course includes doing the middle and lower-level managers' jobs for them). The bit they do shouldn't amount to much. Senior managers do sometimes waste too much of their time on 'retained hobbies' — things they've kept an interest in from their earlier careers. But at their level there's another kind of activity that demands their attention, something that's neither management nor DIY. The managing director of a business organisation has to be more than a bit of an entrepreneur. Besides managing the *organisation* he has to run the *business*. The local government chief officer has to understand the way politicians work. Besides running his department he has to advise councillors on the practical implications of their political intentions. Priorities like these are important and may merge with the management thinking that has to be done at this level. But they aren't *management* priorities.

The point of this detour into the non-management parts of managers' jobs is to clear away the undergrowth and overhanging branches for an unobstructed view of their management role. Now we can concentrate on the management part of the manager's job.

B. The management part

What lies at its core? Although managers' jobs vary enormously, everything they do as managers is summed up in two words: MAKE DECISIONS. Every manager manages by making decisions about the part of the organisation he's been given to manage.

Of course the manager does other things too. He talks and writes and reads and listens and observes and tries to understand what is going on — all the things that are wrapped together in that carpet-bag word 'communicating'. He also walks round the place, he occasionally looks pleased or annoyed, he might even do something now and again to show someone else how — but they're only other forms of communicating. Sometimes he just sits and thinks. But deciding things is what he's there for. All the rest of it is to help him take good decisions and so tell others what he has decided. You could say that thinking and communicating and taking decisions are about all anyone ever does as a manager.

This is as true of a supervisor as it is of a senior manager. The management job of both of them is to make decision after decision after decision — some decisions on big questions, others on small ones. The difference between them is simply the *magnitude of the decisions* they have to take. The biggest decisions in the supervisor's job will be smaller than most of the decisions in the senior manager's job, but they both have to tackle the same kinds of question:

The supervisor asks:
– 'how should our work schedules for the next fortnight be arranged for that heavy workload that's coming?'
– 'how can I help Fred learn how to operate this new machine that's being installed next week?'

The senior manager asks:
– 'how should we plan our activities over the next couple of years to meet the heavy competition?' we're getting?'
– 'how should that new technology be introduced during the next year?'

– 'who's the best worker in my section to handle this tricky assignment?'

– 'who's the best manager we've got to take over the running of that key department?'

– 'what's the best way to get Jane to do her job willingly and well?'

– 'what is the best deal we can negotiate with the Union to prevent these stoppages?'

– 'what can be done about Joe's increasing wastage of materials?'

– 'what can be done about that worrying rise in overhead costs?'

– 'couldn't I delegate this piece of record-keeping to one of my staff?'

– 'shouldn't I make the head of that department responsible for drawing up his own budget?'

Same kinds of question, different magnitudes of decision. And if either the supervisor or the senior manager can't make plans that work, can't pick people well, can't get them to do their jobs effectively and economically, can't delegate properly, it's the same kind of failure. The only difference is the size of the disaster.

Of course, decision-making isn't a prerogative of managers. It's something everyone does all the time. So what's so special about a manager's decisions? The answer is the kinds of questions that his decisions deal with. It's the sorts of thing about which he thinks and communicates and takes decisions that make him a manager. In one way or another they're all governed by the fact that he works in an organisation. So they're all related to those basic features of organisations — the fact that any organisation *does things for a purpose*, the fact that it *has a limited amount of money* to get the things done, the fact that they're done by *people working in groups*.

These things are priorities for the organisation itself and should get attention in the decisions that its managers take. Surprisingly often they don't. That is to say they don't *all* get attention by *all* managers *all* the time. It's a problem of management priorities.

The manager's job

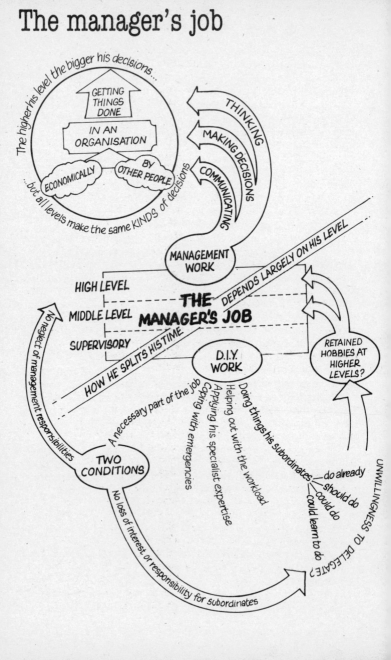

5. Management priorities

When you take decisions, you probably think consciously about the activities that are going on in your area, the way people are working, what you've got to get done, the problems that are hampering getting it done and what you can do to retrieve the situation. Managing anything is a very active occupation, and most of it is a matter of finding practical answers to practical questions: 'how the hell can we get this completed by the deadline?' or 'can I trust Smith to get it right this time?' Now and again you may stand back for a moment and question *why* an activity is done in a certain way — or why it's done at all — or the other possible ways it could be done. In other words you consider aims and think about alternatives.

But the kinds of aims you set and the range of alternatives you consider depend on something much more fundamental in your own thinking. It's your personal orientation that governs the kinds of problems you become aware of, the kinds of questions you ask, the sorts of activity you take an interest in.

Many supervisors and lower-level managers are strongly work-orientated — they're attuned to the practical things that have to be done to get certain results. They're also fairly strongly people-orientated — they're aware of their work forces' attitudes and feelings. But they aren't very economy-minded — they don't see costs in the things they're deciding. Whether there are or aren't any financial angles to be considered isn't the point. *They don't look for them.*

Managers above them tend to be differently orientated. They are result-orientated. They are aware of the output that the sections run by their supervisors and team-leaders produce, but often aren't very interested in what's had to be done to get those results and so aren't attuned to the kinds of practical problems that their decisions on aims and methods can create. They're also cost-orientated. They're sensitive to the spending that's shown in budget returns and other financial documents they see. But their people-orientation is often rather weak. They tend not to notice problems with people's morale or attitudes or abilities because *they don't look for them*.

Each manager's orientation is his in-built sense of what's important — his priorities. Find out what they are and you can tell a lot about his approach to decision-making.

Thinking about what an organisation consists of, what ought to be the priorities for each manager's decisions about his part of it?

1. The WORK it exists to do. Whenever this is a priority for the manager, he thinks in terms of what has to be done, and how and when it has to be done. The problems he sees are those that cause delays or poor quality work. He tries to manage the work so that its output satisfies the purpose of his part of the organisation.

2. The MONEY invested in its resources and the costs of the decisions he makes. Whenever this is a priority for the manager, he thinks in terms of value and expenditure. The problems he sees are those that cause losses or waste. He tries to find productive ways of using his resources and economical ways of gettings things done.

3. The PEOPLE who work there. Whenever they are a priority for the manager, he is not only concerned about the productive use of their time and abilities (which is more a matter of the priority he gives to value-for-money). He also thinks of them as human beings — of their attitudes, their motivation, their working relationships, of what the organisation can offer them as well as what they can offer the organisation. The problems he sees are those of their morale and their interest and ability in what they are doing. He tries to give them positive, caring leadership.

Logically, these three priorities should lie at the core of *every* management job. How the individual manager orders them is a question we'll come to in a moment. First, the range of decisions they give him to take.

The range of management decisions

Decisions are *conscious* choices. Many a manager's failure to make a decision is explained by his not knowing there was a decision to make. Perhaps he was so familiar with the situation and the way things are done that he somehow imagined that there was nothing to be decided. Perhaps he just didn't know what was happening and didn't realise that a decision was needed. It's a different matter if he consciously decided *not* to take a decision — that was a decision in itself, and a real manager won't argue about his responsibility for letting things take their course. But he often feels unfairly criticised when he is taken to task for failing to make a decision that he wasn't aware was there to be taken.

The problem is the range of questions that the manager has to decide. They are so many and so varied that their diversity itself gives him an excuse for missing some of them. But not if he keeps his priorities in mind: they give him a way of categorising the kinds of question he has to keep asking about his operation and his management of it so that nothing important is overlooked.

Decisions about the work

The most immediate decisions that a manager makes are concerned for the most part with *making things happen*. True, some of the decisions that senior managers take about the work may be very long term indeed — decisions on large-scale projects, decisions on major developments in the organisation's operations, decisions on the introduction of new technology and so on. But these kinds of decision don't come every day, and they also raise big questions about the other priorities of finance and human resources. The mass of the decisions that managers take about getting things done are much shorter-term.

Such decisons test your ability to manage the use of *time* —

your people's time and your own. They are the decisions you take on questions like these:

- how much time should I spend in keeping myself informed about the work that is actually going on in my area?
- how can we cope with the workloads we have?
- which are the more important and less important things to get done today? Tomorrow? This week? This month? This year?
- what should be the deadlines for completing our various tasks?
- what quality of result is achievable and acceptable, given the resources I've got?
- how should my staff and equipment be allocated?
- how should we schedule the work?
- what can we do if inputs of materials or information are delayed?
- are our methods of working and the performance of our equipment satisfactory?
- are our systems efficient, and are we identifying properly the exceptions that need special treatment?
- could we get better results if we changed the way we organise the work?
- how can we cope with immediate problems: breakdowns, failures, unexpeced incidents and demands, backlogs of work, outside interference etc?
- what can we do to prevent recurrent problems in the future?
- can we take on further commitments within our present resources?

Lying behind most of these questions is the question of how EFFICIENTLY the work gets done.

Decisions about money

These decisions are often rather longer-term than most of the manager's decisions about the work itself — although obviously, decisions about how to do things will always have some kind of financial effects. But from time to time the manager has to think directly about *getting value for money*. For managers at middle to more senior levels this should be a constant refrain, but the supervisor can't ignore it either. If he and all his supervisor colleagues accept a responsibility to help husband the organisation's resources, they can often make as much impact on the organisation's economy as the rest of its management put together.

Many management decisions test the manager's ability to *avoid waste* — waste of money, waste of time, waste of equipment, waste of materials, waste of people's efforts and capabilities. They are the decisions he takes on questions like these:

- how much time should I spend in trying to understand the financial consequences of the way we operate?
- could I use my people's time and abilities more productively?
- how many staff do we really need to cope with our workloads?
- do we have any highly-paid people doing a lot of low-value work?
- are the methods and systems we use wasteful of time and resources?
- are we wasting money trying to achieve a quality of result that isn't really needed?
- how valid is our budget for the year, and could the actual spending be varied to save money or to get more productive results?
- could we be more economic in our purchase and use of materials? Are we maintaining the most economic stock-levels?
- are we making the most of the accommodation, equipment and services we use?
- could we save money in the long run by spending to improve our resources — getting more efficient equipment, higher-calibre staff, better training, more suitable accommodation?
- should I take greater care over the security of the property and cash in our area?
- are we properly controlling the amount of credit our customers take?
- are our suppliers' invoice and staff expense sheets being checked carefully enough?
- am I getting an adequate return for the organisation from the investment made in that equipment purchase or training programme or sales campaign?
- are we doing things or running up costs that can't be economically justified?
- where can savings be made?
- where can we reduce *waste* — in whatever form it takes? Waste of time? Waste of effort? Waste of peoples' talents and commitment? Waste of anything that represents *value* to the organisation?

Lying behind all these questions is the question of how ECONOMICALLY the organisation's money is being used.

Decisions about people

Many of the management decisions that have the longest-term effects of all are concerned with the *leadership of people*. It's true that a lot of them are taken spontaneously and without much thought for their consequences. They may hardly be decisions at all, but more a manager's spur-of-the-moment reactions to a subordinate's behaviour or to something he has done. The fact that sometimes the manager may afterwards regret his over-hasty reaction isn't perhaps terribly damaging if it doesn't represent his normal way of dealing with human errors and problems with people in his group. But it *is* damaging if he lets his emotions control important decisions like recruitment or promotion or dealing with union demands or coping with the results of poor motivation or low morale. The organisation may have to live with the consequences of those decisions for a long time.

Such decisions test the manager's ability to *understand his people* in the first place — and then his capacity to use that understanding to command their respect and trust, and to build their commitment and their competence in what they are doing. They are the decisions he takes on questions like these:

- how much time should I spend finding out about my people and seeing how they are coping with whatever they are responsible for?
- what relationships should I try to maintain with my subordinates — and with my boss?
- how can I best allocate the work to use each person's capabilities and to give each one a fair workload?
- is everyone clear about the aims we are trying to achieve? Am I myself?
- do they have an adequate idea of the standards of work we should be trying to maintain?
- how should I keep them informed about what's going on generally and of my own intentions for the future in running my part of the organisation?
- are they competent enough to do teir jobs properly and to get a sense of achievement and pride in their work?
- what opportunities could they get to develop their abilities, and to what extent should I be giving them the benefit of my experience?
- what should I delegate and how far can I involve my people?
- does the way we organise our activities and our division of responsibilities enable each of my people to work effectively and to coordinate what he does with what the others are doing?

- are working conditions conducive to good morale?
- are there any risks to health or safety?
- what am I looking for when I recruit new people to my area?
- how should they be introduced to the work they'll be doing and to the people they will be working with?
- how good is the morale and discipline in my area?
- what kinds of things could cause grievances?
- how should I deal with union representatives and the issues which concern them?
- am I doing enough to make my people feel they are part of a team?
- am I using my own abilities and time in the best way?
- what am I doing to develop my own competence as a leader?

Lying behind all these questions is the question of how EFFECTIVELY the organisation's human resources are being used.

Decisions about coordination

In all his decisions on this three key priorities in his own area, the manager has to try to calculate their *effects on other areas* than his own. As a member of an organisation, he can't run his aera as if it were an island unconnected with the rest of the organisation or as though every other area should dance attendance on his own — however important it may be. And it doesn't help if he merely complains about the problems other areas cause him or uses them as an excuse for inefficiencies in his own operation. He has to do something positive to reduce the problems.

This tests the manager's understanding of how this organisation functions as a whole, and his willingness to look beyond narrow self-interest to see how he can best *cooperate* with others. If he takes this view of his role, he will consider questions such as these:

- what relationships should I maintain with other managers whose operations link with my own?
- how much time should I spend in keeping myself informed about their work and the problems they have to contend with, and in informing them about *our* work and problems?
- could this decision I'm about to take have any damaging consequences in their areas?
- are they considering any decisions that could have damaging consequences for our own efficiency, economy or effectiveness?

- how can we alert each other to the need for joint planning of operations and systems?
- how can the links be best maintained — through ad hoc conversations as problems crop up or through regular meetings to try to anticipate the problems?
- what direct access do my subordinates need to people at the same level in these other areas to maintain the detailed coordination that's needed?
- how can I adjust the way my own area is organised so that we can cope better with the unavoidable pressures from other areas?
- where should I accept the transfer of my able people to other areas — and where should I resist it?
- which of my staff have the potential for promotion outside my own area?
- what part can everyone in my area play in enhancing our organisation's reputation with customers and the public generally?

Lying behind all these questions is the question of how well each area CONTRIBUTES to the organisation's total aims.

Perhaps these lists of for-instance questions include many that you feel don't concern you — and you may well be right in a few cases. One or two may simply be inappropriate for the kind of organisation you work in or the bit of it that you're running.

But what about the others? Those that you don't have the power to decide yourself — do you try to help your superiors focus on them when the questions need answering? Those that you might have tried to ask and been told to stop rocking the boat — have you persisted in your efforts to row the damned thing, perhaps in more subtle ways? Those that you haven't ever considered to be your responsibility before now — are you willing to start asking them as a regular part of your management? If you can't answer 'yes' in each case, what in hell's name are you doing in a management job?

Management priorities

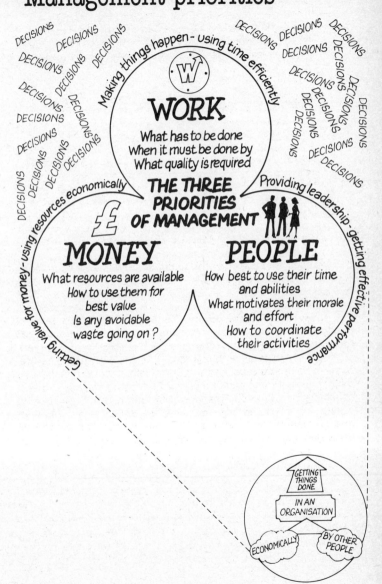

6. Conflicts of priority

A manager can't select which of the three priorities he is responsible for and then make his decisions accordingly. Every real manager feels responsible for *all three* kinds of priority. He accepts responsibility for the WORK that goes on in his area right down to its smallest detail (though he may manage a lot of the detail through his *delegation* which we'll come on to later). He accepts responsibility for the MONEY that's involved in his area or, more accurately, for the balance between its costs, the use of its resources and the value of the work done. He accepts responsibility for the PEOPLE who work for him or his subordinate managers — for their morale, their competence, the use of their time, the direction of their efforts.

Now it's pretty obvious that these things are totally dependent on each other. In practice you can't make a decision about, for example, the deadline for some work that doesn't have some sort of economic effect *and* an effect on the people involved. Any money-type decision you take must have either a direct effect on the work (and so an indirect effect on your people), or a direct effect on your people (and so an indirect effect on their work). A decision for instance on a machine purchase may be made to improve the efficiency of work, but it could also demand staff training to operate the machine — and could even cause fears of redundancy. A decision to give someone a bonus payment could make other staff feel unfairly treated and so cause lower-quality performances from them. And the same principle applies to any people-type decision you make. It cannot help but have an effect on their performance of work and so on their value to your area.

Some so-called managers persist in trying to split the unsplittable. They try to pretend that the performance of work and financial results are all they have to worry about, and kid themselves that the human results of their decisions are no concern of theirs. Or they assume that their role is simply a matter of getting people to do work, supposing that accountants and higher-level managers can 'manage the money'. Very often they'll argue that theirs is a practical approach to the management job. In fact it's pure fantasy. Since their decisions inevitably *do* have an effect on whatever priority they are ignoring, this can only mean that they're willing to let it go on uncontrolled.

The reason why managers try to do these idiotic things is understandable. The most difficult part of any management job is to resolve the conflicts between their priorities — and *conflicts there will be*. If it were actually possible to do what these managers try to maintain and drop one of the priorities overboard, the management job would become far, far simpler. Not easy, even so. But a damn sight easier than it actually is.

Every management decision involves some kind of conflict of priorities, otherwise there would be no decision to make. Simply replace the manager with a computer, feed it all the facts of the situation and the electronics would calculate the right answer. If there's a real decision to take, that's impossible. Computers can only calculate — they can't take decisions. A decision gives you a conflict of priorities which you can resolve only by using your judgement.

What are these conflicts? In any one decision you take, they may be present in various forms. But four kinds of conflicts are common.

A. Conflicts between the priorities

These happen in so many ways that it's difficult to give examples that suggest their range. Just to give some fairly generalised instances more or less at random:

- you have to take a decision on how to get a dull but fairly important job done. What weight should you give to the possible waste of the highly-paid time of fairly high calibre staff on work that isn't up to their abilities? How far should you take into account the need to maintain the interest and involvement of whoever gets the job? And to what extent will these other priorities influence the quality of work you expect in the job and the deadline you set for its completion?
- you have to take a decision on reducing costs in your area. How much thought should you give to the effects on your people's morale and commitment? What weight should you give to the need to retain the productive capacity to cope with future work-loads? And to what extent will these other priorities influence the way in which you try to make the economies?
- you have to take a decision about some training needed by your people. What importance should you give to its costs in time and money and the value of the capabilities it produces? How far can you accept a temporary reduction in the work-capacity of your area, and the following demands on your time to help your people implement what they've learned? And to what extent will these other priorities influence your decision about the quality and thoroughness of the training?

B. Conflicts within each priority

Not only do the priorities conflict with each other, but in many a decision there are conflicts *within* one priority. Work demands conflict with each other. One financial requirement can only be satisfied at the expense of another. You can achieve one purpose with your people only if you let another take a back seat. These conflicts may give you questions such as these to find answers for:
- which of several urgent tasks you have to deal with is the most important to concentrate on?
- is it more important to get a particular job finished on time or to get a high quality result?
- should you press a customer for payment when it means risking the loss of future valuable business?
- should you give an able subordinate a special favour to maintain his motivation if the rest of your people will regard it as being unfair to them?

C. Conflicts between short and longer-term priorities

These are some of the most difficult conflict to resolve. A manager has to keep in mind that he isn't responsible only for what happens today, but also for the performance of his part of the organisation tomorrow and the day after. You can often land yourself in difficulties by the time-honoured method of thinking only of the present and letting the future take care of itself. For instance:

- you may decide on a quick and easy method of getting something done short-term, and then discover it has very wasteful effects in the months to come.
- you may decide to accept a high labour cost for an urgent and important task, and later find you've established an expensive precedent for the future.
- you may decide on a certain system of organising your people's work for the sake of immediate efficiency, but find that in the long term it has damaging consequences in the demotivation and low work-interest it leads to.
- on the other hand, you may decide on a long-term method of developing your people's abilities, and accept the fact that it limits your freedom in the short term to arrange their work in the most cost-effective way.

D. Conflicts with other areas' interests

Yet other conflicts exist between the interests of your own section or department and the interests of other areas of the organisation. These are the conflicts that require decisions about coordination. People who regard each manager's patch as entirely his own concern and no one else's don't see them as anything to bother about in their decision-making. This is a very blinkered view of one's management responsibilities. It ignores the interests of the oganisation as a whole. The good manager tries to see where such conflicts exist and takes them into account in his decisions. For instance:

- your area is causing expensive delays to another manager's operation. You know that to solve the problem you need to change a method of working in your area. But this will cause a temporary disruption to your area at a difficult time. The new method will also cause some increase in your costs, and will involve your people in quite a bit of extra effort. The decision is entirely yours to take. How far will your concern for your own area influence the amount of cooperation you are prepared to give?

– you can overcome a labour difficulty with a current job by agreeing to some extra payments to your staff. As far as your area is concerned, the costs are fully recoverable and will not create a precedent for the future. But it will cause problems in another department also involved with the same job when their staff find out. Their costs are not recoverable. You have complete freedom in making your decision. In taking it, what weight should you give to the other department's interests?

All of these conflicts face every manager with the biggest test of his management ability: HOW TO KEEP HIS PRIORITIES IN PROPER BALANCE. Whether a decision seems to be merely a question of how some work is to be done or how some money is to be saved, it never is *merely* that. It always involves other priorities. And it's no answer to say they're all equally important. The manager can't give them all equal weight in every decision because they're not equally important at the time. Often they *can't* be equally satisfied — something has to take precedence. But that doesn't mean he can safely ignore any of them. They are *priorities* after all, and the question for the manager is what his order of priorities should be in each decision he makes.

Many so-called managers fail the test. Some dodge the priorities they find personally difficult: the need to provide leadership for their people, to maintain good discipline, to achieve high productivity, to help their people grow in ability and competence. Some boil everything down to a few simplistic rules: keep people busy, follow the set procedures, avoid trouble. Some try to ignore the question of priorities altogether — their decision and actions are governed by the latest demand or crisis. Such a 'manager' doesn't manage events or people. They manage *him*.

The effective manager is aware of all the choices that are there for him to make in his moment-by-moment decisions, and he has his balance of priorities thought out in advance as a base for them. As circumstances change he adjusts the way he responds, but his priorities remain. They give him a consistent sense of purpose through all these adjustments, avoiding wild swings and reversals of direction. He is neither too rigid nor over flexible in his approach.

Conflicts of priority

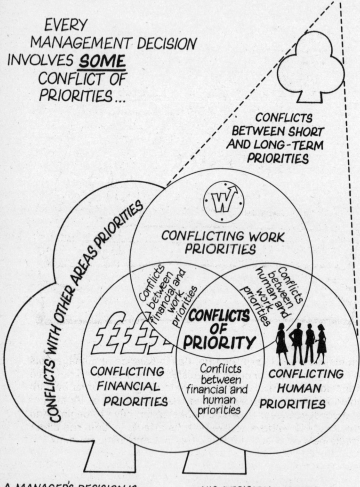

EVERY MANAGEMENT DECISION INVOLVES **SOME** CONFLICT OF PRIORITIES...

CONFLICTS BETWEEN SHORT AND LONG-TERM PRIORITIES

CONFLICTS WITH OTHER AREAS PRIORITIES

CONFLICTING WORK PRIORITIES

Conflicts between financial and work priorities

Conflicts between human and work priorities

CONFLICTS OF PRIORITY

CONFLICTING FINANCIAL PRIORITIES

Conflicts between financial and human priorities

CONFLICTING HUMAN PRIORITIES

A MANAGER'S DECISION IS **HIS** WAY OF RESOLVING THE CONFLICTS HE IS AWARE OF...

...HIS DECISION-MAKING TESTS HIS ABILITY TO **KEEP HIS PRIORITIES IN PROPER BALANCE**

7. Resolving the conflicts

Difficult as it is to keep the priorities in balance, a manager has one thing to help him in each decision he makes: the time scale of the decision. This is a question of looking at the urgency with which its results are needed and the importance of its longer-term consequences. How soon does action have to begin? And how long will he have to live with its effects — both the direct effects he's after and the side-effects it may have for him?

A. The time-scales of management decision-making

The higher a manager's level, the bigger are the effects of the decisions he takes and the more difficult it is to get each decision right. The difference between the supervisor's decisions and those taken by the head of a big department is a difference in the scope of the work that their decisions control, in the amounts of money involved, in the numbers of people affected and in the importance of the outcome.

But this isn't all. There's a difference too in the TIME-SCALES of the effects of the decisions — or rather of those effects that the decision-maker could be expected to *foresee*. Suppose we're looking at the decision-making in a fairly simple organisation with three levels of management: supervisor, department head and chief executive.

Most of the supervisor's decisions are for today — to be put into action within minutes or hours. Many are for action over the next few days, some for action next week or next month. The longest-term decision he can take might be for results up to three months on from today. Beyond that, the effects of any decision he makes now will have been overtaken by events or by his department head's decisions, so he can't feel personally responsible for any longer-term consequences.

The department head has several supervisors reporting to him. He doesn't want to interfere with their decisions for the immediate future, and in any case he needs to think longer-term than this. So he tries to avoid having to get involved in deciding what's to be done this week or next. Only in an emergency do any of his decisions have to be acted on that quickly. In the normal way of things, his shortest-term decisions are for action in two weeks' time and onwards, and he expects his supervisors to coordinate *their* decisions for action that far ahead with his own decisions. Much of what he decides will take months to implement — perhaps even a year or more. But like the supervisors, he can't feel responsible for the consequences beyond a certain point — say eighteen months ahead.

The chief executive links his department heads' decision-making with his own in the same way. Emergency decisions for him are those that would have to be acted on within the next couple of months or so, and so he tries to avoid the need for them. He has to give himself time for thinking about the long-term future and deciding what is to happen in his organisation next year and the year after, up to say four or five years on from today. The decisions he takes on his normal time-scale begin to take effect in say two to three months' time and onwards. So the way these three divide their responsibilities for decision-making might look like this:

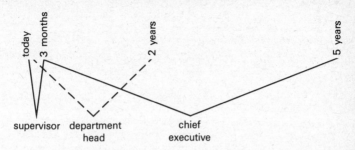

Time into the future

today — 3 months — 2 years — 5 years

supervisor — department head — chief executive

That's how it *ought* to work — but usually doesn't. What actually happens in many organisations is that those emergency decisions become the norm for the middle and senior managers. Often it's because they're failing to delegate properly. Often it's because they're not keeping their subordinates at the next level down sufficiently in the picture about the longer-term needs they themselves can foresee, about their future intentions, about the decisions they are taking. Often it's because their subordinates are inadequately selected or trained to get their own shorter-term decisions right.

Whatever the reason, the senior manager frequently gets himself involved in short-term decision-making for action this month, this week. This has two effects. In the first place, it means that he now hasn't got the time for thinking about the long-term future: the decisions that he *ought* to be making for next year and the year after *aren't* being made. In the second place, it puts considerable pressure on the middle-level managers also to get involved in decision-making for this week, even for today — and *their* longer-term decision-making isn't getting done.

Where does this leave the supervisors? Trying to change yesterday of course! The whole organisation is managed by a series of crises. And the culprits are managers who can't delegate, who won't communicate properly with their subordinates, who can't be bothered to pick their subordinates wisely and to see they develop the abilities and kinds of managerial thinking that are needed. They turn the job of managing their organisation into a mass of problem-solving activities because they lack the ability to order their priorities.

B. The time-scales of the priorities

Now look again at those priorities — work, money and people. Like the decisions of managers at the different levels, they have different time-scales too.

Taking the broad view, most of a manager's decisions about getting *work* done are shorter-term than his decisions about the other priorities, *and they can be changed more rapidly*. Because he has decided to do something one way this week doesn't limit his freedom to decide to do it another way next week as far as the work is concerned. What may restrict him is the willingness and ability of his people to change their way of doing it, because they take longer to change. Because he has decided to start a project this month doesn't limit his freedom to cancel it next month as far as the project itself is concerned. What is likely to restrict him is the waste of money and resources that would be involved in the aborted project.

Decisions about the *use of money* tend to have rather longer-term consequences that generally can't be changed so readily without damaging effects. Sudden 'economy drives' may sometimes be needed to rescue organisations from financial crises (that they shoudn't have gotten into in the first place). But their most common result in the short term is that the money that remains in circulation is now used in *less* effective and *less* economic ways than it was being used before. They throw the balance of the priorities out of gear. They also get managers into the way of thinking that unless there's a special drive on, economy isn't important. To prevent the need for such drives, decisions about finance often need to anticipate events further ahead than do decisions about operations.

The longest-term effects of all can stem from decisions about *people*. Poor morale and a bad atmosphere among the people working in an organisation can take years of management effort to overcome. The decisions involved in tackling people-problems are both major and long-term. So are decisions about the organisation's structure or the recruitment of people into it or the development of managers' abilities. If people's roles and relationships are changed, it takes time for them to become fully effective in the new arrangement, to learn how to cope with altered roles and to get used to working with each other in unaccustomed ways. A decision to employ someone, even in a comparatively junior position, can commit the organisation to a bigger cost in his pay over the years than a decision on a major project or on buying several large pieces of equipment. If it's a more senior manager who's being recruited, you can add to his even larger salary bill the costs, in human and financial terms, of all the decision-making *he'll* be doing over the years to come. And if a number of managers in an organisation aren't doing their jobs effectively, it may take several years of training and development to give them the competence they need.

Yet many of these far-reaching decisions are taken with less care than quite minor decisions about work or money. A department may go through reorganisation after reorganisation, often only months apart, as bright ideas about its structure occur to the manager in charge of it — or perhaps because he has got a low threshhold of boredom! An important management appointment may be made after a few sociable chats that pass for 'interviews' and on the basis of totally inadequate knowledge of the real requirements of the job that has to be filled. An ineffectual manager is often sent off on a three-day course in the belief that this alone will cure the problem.

The fact remains. Decisions like these about people and their coordination and training are major decisions. Their consequences have very long time-scales indeed, often far longer than the time-scales of decisions about the organisation's finances.

What this is saying is that if an organisation isn't to be managed largely by emergency-type decisions, managers need to tackle the right sorts of question far enough ahead. Management isn't setting things in motion and then waiting for the crunch. It means taking decisions in advance of the crunch to prevent it happening. To do this, management priorities have to be ordered to suit each manager's level in the organisation and the time-spans over which his decisions operate.

Now there's nothing new in the idea that a manager's level decides his priorities. It has been a part of conventional thinking about management for a long time. So why are so many organisations dealing almost constantly with emergencies of one sort or another, their managers running from one problem to the next? The reason is the way that priorities are ordered by the conventional idea of management hierarchy.

C. The conventional order of priorities

This says that supervisors and managers live in two different worlds. One is the world of the workforce in which the supervisor lives — a world where people live for today with little thought for tomorrow. They are concerned with activity and doing things, with wages and spending them, with job security, with satisfactions outside work. The supervisor shares these attitudes and interests because he has usually been promoted from the workforce. He looks at his organisation and its management from the workers' point of view. So the supervisor's priorities are simple and practical — his people and the work they do. The treatment the workforce receives is his responsibility. For the work he's a progress-chaser, a passer-on of management's instructions, a solver of immediate problems. Finance and economy aren't his business (apart from keeping his people busy). They're for managers to worry about.

The conventional idea also says that the manager's world is one the workforce and its supervisors couldn't understand even if they tried to. It's a world of aims and objectives, of costs and profitability, of markets and competition, of technology and productivity, of figures and paperwork, of organisational politics and power-games. Its people think about the future and the fulfilment of their ambitions. They gain their satisfactions through personal achievement and the development of their careers. They are planners and policy-makers, concerned about financial angles in anything they have to deal with. Whether the mass of managers actually operate in this way isn't the point. It's the conventional idea of the way managers ought to operate and it shapes their priorities.

So it forces on the manager two priorities in running his area of the organisation. First, its output or whatever results it is supposed to achieve (the actual work that people do to achieve this output is of little concern to him unless it produces unsatisfactory results). Secondly, the financial effects of its operations and the costs of the resources it uses. The more senior he is, the more likely it is that money becomes his over-riding concern. The organisation's people in general rank rather low in his order of priorities, and the workforce hardly rates at all. He doesn't need to get involved in the practical details of how they do things or of the way they're treated unless supervisory failures force him to.

This case may be over-stated, and many managers would vehemently deny that they operate this way. But it's a picture of management that constantly surfaces in books, journals, conferences, seminars, public debates and other places where management thinking is aired. It's visible in organisation structures and job descriptions and management development programmes. Managers reveal it in their actions and behaviour. And wherever it reaches it causes bad spirit, low work-standards, inefficiency and waste. Waste of people's potential, waste of efforts, waste of time, waste of money.

That's the inevitable result of this conventional sheep-and-goats idea about management and the workforce. It's almost bound to happen if managers ignore *how the work is actually done* in their areas of responsibility and dump most of the practical decisions about the treatment of the workforce on to supervisors. Apart from questions of staff numbers, pay levels and union negotiations (where supervisors' views are rarely even asked for), many managers get involved in decisions about their workforces only if there's a problem of some sort. On the other hand they assume that it's possible to keep all the financial decisions to themselves and the accountants — forgetting that supervisors' decisions can waste money unawares. New thinking is needed to get managers to pay attention to the wasteful and demoralising problems that so often occur at the working level — and that are even *caused* by their own decision-making.

D. A new order of priorities

The way managers order their priorities at each level should depend on the kind of decisions that are most important at their level, and the time it takes for those decisions to get results — the 'lead-time' of the decisions. Now it's generally true that small decisions can have short lead-times and big decisions need long lead-times. But it doesn't always follow. Rome wasn't built in a day — but it *could* have been built in, say a few months if limitless money and people with the skills and organisation to do it were freely available. As we've seen, the lead-time of a decision is generaly governed by the kind of priority it is most concerned with — work, money or people:

- decisions in which the priority is the WORK to be done generally need little lead-time. They can be quickly implemented and their results are soon evident.
- decisions in which the priority is MONEY, its availability and economy in using it generally need longer lead-times to implement. It may take several months or more before their effects produce a pay-off.
- decisions in which PEOPLE'S attitudes, abilities and working relationships are the priority usually need the longest lead-times of all. They may take years to achieve the intended results.

For example, let's look at a hotel manager who's considering changing the system by which his reception staff checks in guests. His priorities in making this decision will depend on the kind of change he's thinking of. Whatever the priority is will affect the lead-time of his decision:

IF HIS PRIORITY IS THE WORK ITSELF:

> –the aim is to improve only the efficiency with which guests are dealt with as they arrive: it will mean quicker checking-in, or fewer mistakes in connecting an advance booking with the guest who has just arrived.

Suppose that this is the only question involved in the decision — that there are no effects on finance or staff that the manager needs to concern himself with. Then it will take no longer to implement than it takes to give instructions to the staff and (say) to print new booking-in forms. A lead-time of perhaps a week or so?

IF HIS PRIORITY IS FINANCIAL ECONOMY:

> –the change aims to economise in staff time: this will make it possible to deal with larger numbers of guests expected in the future without increasing staff.
> –the change involves buying new equipment: the cost will take some time to recoup.

Suppose these are the key questions involved. Obviously it is going to take rather longer to reach a pay-off than to achieve just the increased efficiency of the work priority. A lead-time of perhaps two or three months?

IF HIS PRIORITY IS THE EFFECTIVENESS OF HIS STAFF:

> –the change is one that requires reception staff to develop new abilities: it will involve training and an initial period of operation when they are *less* efficient than before. It may even require a higher calibre of staff.
> –the success of the change depends on the staff's willingness to make it work: it will upset working relationships that they are used to and enjoy. They may be worried about redundancies.
> –the change may affect the attitudes staff show towards guests: if morale suffers, the hotel's reputation may be damaged by indifferent or surly attitudes in reception.

Suppose these kinds of issues are involved. To prepare staff in a way that avoids problems of attitude and morale and to get them to the point where they are operating a new system with skill and ease may take a considerable time. A lead-time of perhaps five or six months or more?

This question of the required lead-time obviously applies to the different decisions that a single manager may take. But on a broader scale, it also governs the order of priorities for managers working at different levels in an organisation. Try looking at it from the point of view of each of the three managers we considered a few pages back: the supervisor, the department head, and the chief executive.

You're the supervisor . . . Your management decisions have short lead-times. Hours, days, a few weeks at the most.

Your first priority is the efficiency of the work you're responsible for and the time available for its performance. This is the first thing to consider when you schedule tasks and allocate them to your people. A lot of your decisions *are* problem-solving — sorting out hitches that are causing delays or backlogs or poor quality work. But you'll have fewer problems to solve if you've developed habits of looking forward when you take decisions about the work and try to anticipate difficulties in the work-flow. You can probably foresee such problems in more practical terms than the managers above you can.

Your people probably rank next in your order of priorities. You don't take the bigger, longer-term decisions that affect their general attitude to the organisation or their use of their capabilities. But you do influence their morale by the relationship you maintain with them, and by the ways you deal with immediate problems in their job performance and their discipline. You, more than any 'higher level' of manager, are in a position to know and understand how your people's motivations and interests are moving. That knowledge needs to be relayed to those above you for use in *their* longer-term decisions affecting your people.

The economy of your operation ranks third in your priorities, not because you should be less concerned about it, but because you can't do so much to influence it. Your decisions don't have the scope to tackle the bigger financial issues and you probably don't have the authority or knowledge either. But economy's not unimportant, even at your level. Working methods that waste efforts, materials or time, under-employed staff, risks of costly accidents — you're often the only manager who's directly aware of such things, and many of them can be controlled by the decisions you take. If higher-level decisions are needed to prevent any waste you can see going on but can't actually do anything to stop, *your* decision is to keep your boss informed.

You're the department head . . . Your management decisions have lead-times of weeks, months, up to a year or so — which is about the period over which realistic financial plans can be made.

Money is your first priority, in other words the cost-effectiveness and economy of your decisions. Actual money-values are the basis for a lot of your decision-making-budgets and cash-flows, the costs of people and the value of their work. But many of the values your decisions have to take into account *can't* be directly measured in pounds and pence: the productivity of your department, the capabilities of its work-force, the effectiveness of its supervisors and other managers, the coordination of the different departmental activities. Such things have an obvious influence on the cost-effectiveness that your decisions must achieve, so you can't limit yourself to a narrow accountancy view of finance.

The actual work that goes on in the department probably wins second place by a short head in your order of priorities. Your budget doesn't mean much without the plan of physical activities that it pays for. Financial economy doesn't come into question until you have operations to run. Though the actions you decide are on a bigger scale than those of your supervisors, they still require attention to the detail of what you actually expect people to do. This makes your link with your supervisors a crucial one — because of the knowledge you can get by discussing how the work is going and by listening to their problems and ideas. But this knowledge alone isn't enough. You need to supplement it by what you can find out for yourself from regular walkabouts in your department, eyes and ears open.

The priority you give to the department's human resources ranks third only on the assumption that your supervisors are effective leaders and that your chief executive treats people as *his* first priority. If this isn't so, you have to give people's morale and effectiveness a higher priority in your own decisions.

You're the chief executive . . . Your management decisions have longer lead-times than any other decisions taken in the organisation — up to several years ahead. So a key question for you is how effectively your organisation will be able to cope with the longer-term future. Your decisions are concerned with major changes and how to bring them about. If you or your predecessors have made some duff decisions in the past, the organisation may need some big changes to cope successfully with present-day circumstances. In any case, to hold its own in the world of five or ten years ahead (or however far forward your vision reaches) you know it will have to change: its markets or the public it serves will change; the demands on it will change; its technology will change; its financial structure will change; its operations will change.

And so its people will have to change. Your organisation's people and the way they are organised are your first priority in the management decisions you must take to make the changes happen. Not just its senior managers and the up-and-coming youngsters who'll replace them in the future, important as they are. The changes your decisions will need to generate are changes in the organisation's human resources generally: workforce, union relationships, supervision, specialists, departmental managers . . . And changing people is a slow business. So your decisions are most often concerned with long-term strategies — strategies to create new abilities in the workforce and among management, to reshape organisational structures, to evolve different staffing arrangements, to get acceptance of different personnel policies.

This makes money your *second* priority, not your first. If the organisation's people have really been the first priority of top management for long enough, you'll have department heads who make costs and money-values *their* first priority. Certainly, financial considerations weigh heavily in your decisions for the next year or two. But if you make long-term decisions with human resources as your first priority, you or your successors won't have to be constantly taking emergency decisions in the future to stop the organisation going bust.

Now and again, you may take a decision on the way something downstairs in the organisation is to be done — one in which the priority is the work itself rather than the finance or people involved. But that's likely to be a rare decision for you unless you have incompetent department heads and supervisors, and whose fault is that?

Of course if your organisation is a business, all of this ignores the role in which you make decisions as a businessman rather than as a manager. Wearing that particular hat, you *do* concentrate on operational and financial decisions about what the business will do to retain its markets, increase its market share, maintain its profitability, secure adequate capital and so on — preferably long-term decisions rather than short-term for the sake of your management hat. But these involve business priorities, not management priorities.

Resolving the conflicts

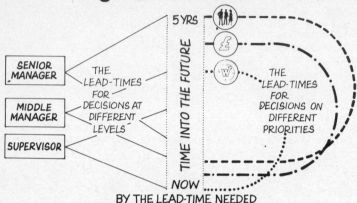

5 YRS

TIME INTO THE FUTURE

THE LEAD-TIMES FOR DECISIONS AT DIFFERENT LEVELS

THE LEAD-TIMES FOR DECISIONS ON DIFFERENT PRIORITIES

SENIOR MANAGER

MIDDLE MANAGER

SUPERVISOR

NOW

BY THE LEAD-TIME NEEDED
FOR DECISIONS TO TAKE EFFECT

⇧

RESOLVING THE CONFLICTS

⇩

A LOGICAL ORDER OF THE PRIORITIES AT EACH LEVEL

The priorities for up to a month or two ahead	The priorities for the next year or so	The priorities for the long-term future

THE SUPERVISOR

1. The efficiency of work and the time available for it.
2. The day-to-day treatment of the workforce.
3. Avoiding waste of the given resources.

THE MIDDLE MANAGER

1. Economy and cost-effectiveness in using resources.
2. The organisation of work and its standards.
3. The abilities of people at lower levels.

THE SENIOR MANAGER

1. The development and organisation of human **RESOURCES**.
2. The availability of resources and their **ALLOCATIONS**.
3. Future changes in the organisation's **OPERATIONS**.

8. Delegating the decision-making

No manager, whatever his level, is humanly capable of making all the decisions for the part of the organisation he runs. Some he can't take because he hasn't the authority: they're the decisions that managers above him take and require him to implement in his own shorter-term decision-making. Others are best taken by his subordinates: decisions that are more relevant to their priorities than to his; decisions whose practical consequences can be better foreseen at a lower level in the organisation; decisions with lead-times so short he wouldn't even know they were needed until too late. Some of the most important of a manager's decisions are to do with the freedom he allows his subordinates to do things in their own way. *He* decides what to let *them* decide.

DELEGATION is the name given to this process of deciding-what-to-let-your-subordinates-decide. It's the one ability more than any other that makes managers different from non-managers. Managers know the difference between *delegating* and *dumping*. Non-managers don't. They think that delegation is giving people things to do, or handing jobs over to people and then forgetting them — the jobs that is. Some even forget the people too.

A common misunderstanding is to think of delegation only as the act of creating a new task in a subordinate's job. The decisions a subordinate makes as part of his normal work aren't thought of as delegated, so that when managers are asked about their delegation they say they can't delegate anything because their subordinates have enough to do as it is. Which puts them in the same league as the fat lady who thought the diet her doctor had prescribed was to be taken between her normal meals.

A manager's delegation covers every decision his subordinates make about the work and resources they control and (if they themselves are managers) about their treatment of their people. If there's anything they decide that he's not treating as delegation, he's dumping it.

If you're a manager, you know how to delegate properly. If you're an experienced manager, you're doing it so consistently that it has gone beyond simple knowledge. You've developed ingrained habits of getting it right. Each time you do it, you no more need to think about how you're doing it than you need to think about how to keep your balance when you walk. But anyone who's just learning to walk in management has consciously to practise the fundamentals of delegation that the old hands may hardly be aware they're using:

- the principle of responsibility.
- the principle of authority.
- the principle of accountability.

A. The principle of management responsibility

This principle says that if you're a manager, you accept a personal responsibility for anything that happens in the part of the organisation you've been given to manage. But as a manager you've delegated to your subordinates a lot of the decisions that affect each of these priorities. So how can you still be responsible for them? This is where you've got a problem with the word 'responsibility' and the different ways it's used.

In one sense, 'responsibility' can mean that you have caused or allowed something to happen, whether on purpose or not. A car driver might admit to being 'responsible' for an accident; a terrorist might claim to be 'responsible' for a murder. But all they mean is that they accept that they caused it — whether by negligence or bad luck in the one case or deliberate intent on the other.

For the manager, 'responsibility' means more than this. It means that he *accepts a duty to take care of something* — and the 'something' may not be entirely in his control. If parents are said to be 'responsible' for their children's behaviour, it doesn't mean that they personally cause it. They have a duty to try to control it — or more accurately, to help their children learn self-control. They can be held to blame if their children behave badly *even in the parents' absence.*

In the same way, the manager is responsible for everything he has delegated to his subordinates. If they themselves are managers, he will have delegated to them, for instance, a responsibility for productivity and morale in their areas. *They* accept a duty to take care of these things (if they don't, he can't delegate). But he still has a duty to see that they do take care of them. The same goes for the decisions they take on anything else. He can be held to blame if his subordinates make a mess of things, even when he isn't there — and he won't be there for most of the time if he's delegating properly.

Every manager is responsible for decisions he didn't take and actions he didn't perform. This implies that he knows what he's letting himself in for — that he knows what it feels like to find a subordinate has made a bad decision and to have to say 'I accept the responsibility'. It's not a simple piece of knowledge that he can get from being told what the responsibility is or from observing others coping with it. The sense of what one is taking on in a responsibility develops with experience. It has got to be *learned.*

B. The principle of management authority

To manage well, any manager whatever his level must feel he has a *right* to manage the things he's responsible for. The feeling is created by the very fact that he has accepted the responsibility. He feels that gives him a personal right to make decisions about the part of the organisation he's been given to manage. But feeling that you have a right to make decisions isn't enough. As a manager, your right to make them has to be accepted by everyone else in the organisation.

Authority is rather like management itself in the sense that management is something you do, not merely something you are. That works for authority too. It's something you *use,* not merely something you *have.* If everyone accepts that you have authority over something or someone, then you mustn't duck taking the decisions you ought to take and have the right to take. That would be 'dereliction of duty' in the military phrase.

Whether he takes them himself or delegates them, every manager has an obligation to see that the decisions that are necessary in his area are taken. If the manager accepts the responsibility for his area, he has a duty to use his authority to manage it.

This is an idea that causes problems for a lot of young managers, and many older ones too. It's a word problem again. They translate 'authority' to mean 'power over other people', thinking presumably of the school-teachers of their youth and the police and other authority figures. Some rather like this idea. Given authority they treat it as a licence to throw their weight around and generally behave like the archetypal school bully. Others loathe the idea and try to get as far as possible from it by avoiding unpleasant decisions and being particularly nice to their people. Both the bully and the nice guy fail in their different ways to use their management authority effectively because they misunderstand what it's all about.

For the manager, his 'authority' means *the right to have his decisions acted on*. The most important person to accept this right of the manager is his boss — simply because the boss has the responsibility for the things the manager decides. When the boss delegates authority to his subordinate managers, it means that he gives them some of his own rights to decide things. It also means that he promises not to interfere in the decisions he's delegated, and undertakes to do his damndest to stop anyone *else* in the organisation from interfering. If he delegates the freedom to decide things, he's also got to support his subordinate managers' *use* of that freedom.

So there's an essential difference between what happens when responsibility is delegated and when authority is delegated. When a manager delegates responsibility for something, he's still responsible for it. When he delegates authority, he loses his right to make the decisions involved. Many managers find this a difficult idea to grasp. It's easiest to see how the principle works in delegating a responsibility for money:

> A manager is responsible for doing something that involves spending up to say £1000. He himself is given the authority to spend that amount. He has three subordinates to whom he delegates parts of the responsibility, and to each one he gives authority to spend up to £300 of the total sum. First question: how much spending is he now responsible for? Answer: £1000. Next question: how much spending has he now the authority to decide? Answer: £100.

And the same principle applies to anything else he delegates to his subordinates: their authority to control the work done in their areas of responsibility, their authority to manage their people, their authority to arrange coordination. He's given the *authority* to them, but he's still got the *responsibility* for the way they use it.

The manager doesn't delegate authority just because he's kind-hearted towards his subordinates. He delegates it because he's *got* to if he wants to do his own management job properly. He's got to for two reasons. One is that he can't possibly take all the decisions. If he tries to he'll get many of them wrong because he hasn't the time to consider them properly nor the time to get all the information they should be based on. The other reason is that unless his subordinates have authority, they can't feel responsible. Authority and responsibility go together.

But the manager has to *specify* the authority he delegates. His subordinates have to know how far they can go — what they can decide and what they can't. He can't simply let them feel they can take decisions about anything they take it into their heads to feel personally responsible for. That way lies organisational chaos. He has to *limit* their authority so that they don't unwittingly take decisions that foul up other things he's responsible for or that conflict with his *own* decisions.

Authority is delegated in this way right down through the organisation from level to level. At every level, each manager delegates a part of his own authority to his subordinate managers. If he's a manager, he'll see they are clear about the authority they've got and where the limits lie. If he's not, his subordinates will have to find out for themselves by getting their bottoms kicked when they don't take decisions they ought to take or when they go too far.

To a certain extent, each manager's authority is restricted by other things. The unwritten laws that govern peoples' expectations and behaviour throughout the organisation are one thing. People outside the manager's own patch are another: other managers whose operations are affected by the decisions he takes for his own operation; specialists like accountants and industrial relations people who help in different ways to coordinate the organisation's money-management and people-management.

But apart from the limits his boss imposes, the biggest constraint of all on the manager's own authority is often his own people down the line. He can take whatever decisions he likes about what they should do and how they should do it, but the decisions are pointless if they don't accept his authority. His boss may say he's delegated it, but the manager hasn't got it in practice.

The problem may be one the manager creates for himself. Perhaps his leadership is weak. Perhaps his decisions are foolish. Perhaps his subordinates can see better than he can what the decisions ought to have been. The problem may be one that someone else has created for him. Perhaps a non-manager above him is failing in *his* responsibility to support the manager's own authority. Perhaps the whole show has been handed over to union militants by non-managers in the past. But the principle still stands: a manager has authority to manage his people only to the extent that they accept his authority. He can try forcing them to accept it — on occasions perhaps he *must* do so. But if he's constantly managing them in that way, what does it do for their morale and his leadership? No, his authority has to be *earned*.

C. The principle of management accountability

This is the principle that makes the other two work. It's also the most neglected of the three. Countless non-managers in management jobs insist that they're delegating when all they're doing is dumping responsibilities and authority on to their subordinates. That isn't delegation. It doesn't become delegation until the subordinates are made accountable for what they do with their authority.

Unlike his responsibilities and authority, a manager's accountability doesn't depend on him. His responsibilities don't exist unless he accepts them. His authority doesn't exist unless he exercises it. But he has no choice over his accountability — that's something his boss demands of him in return for the authority the boss has delegated. The manager can be held accountable for anything he has authority over. Accountability is his boss's *right to know.*

So it's up to the boss to make the manager accountable for the decisions he makes about his part of the organisation. In other words, accountability should match authority. If it doesn't, authority is being dumped, not delegated.

To see how the principle works, suppose you're a manager somewhere in an organisation, say a manager of a unit with several section heads reporting to you. Your responsibility for the unit embraces the sections run by your subordinates of course — you're responsible for seeing that everything is properly run.

But naturally, you've delegated to them authority over their own sections. As a good manager you avoid interfering with their decisions unnecessarily. Anyway you can't be there all the time because that would be bad for their management and yours. Your absence gives them a greater feeling of freedom and responsibility and it gives you time to attend to your other management work.

How do you avoid the risks of dumping? You can't feel responsible if you don't know what's going on, and you can't even take sensible decisions yourself about your unit as a whole. Perhaps your section heads are having trouble with the work or the people they're responsible for. Perhaps they're over-reaching their authority. Perhaps they're acting quite properly within their authority but their decisions have side-effects on things you're responsible for elsewhere. They don't know that. If you knew what was happening you'd play your hand differently, but *you don't know either.*

As a good manager you don't run into this problem because you've made your section heads accountable to you. To keep yourself informed on the things you need to know for your own management of the unit, you've got them reporting to you on those things at regular intervals. That's how accountability can be made to work.

If managers aren't making their subordinates accountable, its usually pretty obvious (although presumably not to the managers concerned). The manager who's the problem is the one who makes his subordinates only partially accountable. He really gums up the works because his dumping isn't so obvious. He wants to be kept informed about the progress of their work and its results, but doesn't want to know about their people's productivity or the state of their morale. He requires details of costs and why the money was spent, but ignores the problems of coordination and the larger amounts of money they waste.

It doesn't help him to assume that "my subordinates will tell me if there's anything else I ought to know". That's putting the boot on the wrong foot. It's asking his subordinates to decide what they are accountable for, and how the hell are they supposed to know if he doesn't tell them? They don't have his responsibilities or his wider view of what's going on, so they can only guess what information might be relevant to him. Nor do they have any particular responsibility to rescue him from the consequences of his dumping.

Accountability is rather like authority in reverse. In exactly the same way that authority is delegated down through the organisation, accountability is maintained upwards from level to level. The manager at the top holds the senior managers who report to him accountable for everything he's given them authority to decide, including *their* decisions about what to delegate and how. That puts pressure on the senior managers to make their subordinate managers in the middle levels accountable to *them* — otherwise they can't account for the things they've delegated to their subordinates . . . and so on down the line.

The rule isn't an absolute one. You might be a supervisor who's had things dumped on you by a non-manager above you. If he doesn't maintain your accountability to him, that's his affair. You can still act like a manager and insist that your subordinates keep you informed. As a manager yourself, you have a right to know.

Many a young manager thinks that being a good delegator is primarily to do with finding new things to delegate to his people. That's not unimportant — people need opportunities to try taking on new responsibilities. It's the way *they* grow in ability and experience, and often enough a way for their manager to test *his* managerial good judgement (is he delegating the right things to the right people in the right way?) and to free himself from unnecessary DIY. But it's not the most important part of delegation.

The good delegator is marked out by the way he maintains his delegation of the responsibilities his people have *already* got. He's the manager who encourages his subordinates to develop a fuller sense of responsibility for those things, a better understanding of what's involved. He refuses to be pushed into interference with the freedom of action — the authority — he has delegated to them. Except in a dire emergency he tries to get them to sort out their problems for themselves, to take their own decisions and to learn from the experience of having to correct their own errors of judgement. But equally importantly he insists on his right to be kept informed about what is going on — he maintains their accountability to him.

Not only does he do this himself. He also does everything in his power to prevent his superiors from interfering with the things he has delegated — if they have tendencies that way.

Delegating the decision-making

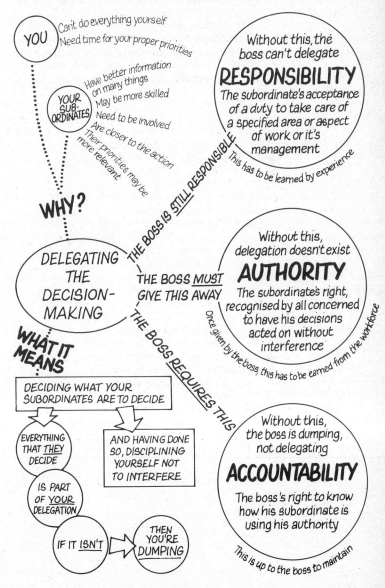

YOU — Can't do everything yourself / Need time for your proper priorities

YOUR SUB-ORDINATES — Have better information on many things / May be more skilled / Need to be involved / Are closer to the action / Their priorities may be more relevant

WHY?

DELEGATING THE DECISION-MAKING

THE BOSS IS _STILL RESPONSIBLE_

THE BOSS _MUST_ GIVE THIS AWAY

THE BOSS _REQUIRES_ THIS

Without this, the boss can't delegate
RESPONSIBILITY
The subordinate's acceptance of a duty to take care of a specified area or aspect of work or it's management

This has to be learned by experience

Without this, delegation doesn't exist
AUTHORITY
The subordinate's right, recognised by all concerned to have his decisions acted on without interference

Once given by the boss, this has to be earned from the workforce

WHAT IT MEANS

DECIDING WHAT YOUR SUBORDINATES ARE TO DECIDE

EVERYTHING THAT _THEY_ DECIDE

AND HAVING DONE SO, DISCIPLINING YOURSELF NOT TO INTERFERE

IS PART OF _YOUR_ DELEGATION

IF IT _ISN'T_ → THEN YOU'RE DUMPING

Without this, the boss is dumping, not delegating
ACCOUNTABILITY
The boss's right to know how his subordinate is using his authority

This is up to the boss to maintain

9. The experienced bad manager

Like those of us know who've tried walking on stilts, it's one thing to understand a principle but it's another thing entirely to make it work in practice. Read any book about management and you might come to the same conclusion. 'Put like that' you might say, 'it's just common-sense. But it's bloody difficult to put into practice when you've got your boss at you for some urgent work that your staff are busy making a mess of, and there are a couple of important visitors waiting for you in your office, and the health and safety representative is pressing you to do something about those dangerous steps in No. 3 workshop and threatening to call in the factory inspector if you don't act quick.' When you're in a situation like that, theory goes out of the window I'll grant you. You just do the best you can, using whatever management abilities you already have. The middle of a storm at sea isn't the time to try to improve your navigation skills.

But how did you get to be a manager in the first place? Not how did you get the position, but what turned you into a manager? You haven't always been one, so somewhere something happened that gave you the ability to manage. You'd impressed someone enough to give you a job that involved managing something, and then what? It wasn't a skill you'd picked up by watching the kinds of things managers do, because most of the skills aren't visible — they go on in managers' heads. Nor could you learn it by attending courses or reading books, no more than you could learn seamanship or piano-playing.

In any case most of the ability isn't simply a knowledge of principles. It's more a matter of learning how to think and behave in management situations and getting enough practical experience of management to make those ways of thinking and behaving more or less second nature. Experience has to be the manager's teacher. There's no other way of learning the 'feel' of management other than by doing it.

But a lot depends on what you mean by 'experience'. It seems to be a general assumption that so many years of experience of doing something automatically make anyone competent, capable, skilled and all the other good things in proportion to the years he has done it for. If X years of doing it gives anyone Y competence, then 2X years gives him 2Y competence. That ain't necessarily so and the evidence is all around if we look for it, rather than taking anyone's statements about his experience at face value.

Take that meeting you went to last week. A model of how *not* to run a meeting, but the chairman had ten years' experience — of running bad meetings. Or that course you attended a few months ago. Boring and parts of it were incomprehensible, but the tutor had fifteen years' experience — of running bad courses. And the same applies wherever you look — experienced bad shop-assistants, experienced bad garage-mechanics, experienced bad waiters . . . The problem doesn't respect the professions: doctors, teachers, accountants, architects and all the others can be as bad in their chosen vocations even with years of so-called experience. Managers aren't immune either. Some of the worst have had the longest experience in management jobs.

The problem is caused by a general confusion between experience and time-serving. If experience means anything worthwhile, it means constantly trying to do the thing better.

The truly experienced performer in any field has reached his present competence by a long history of never being satisfied that he was doing it as well as he could have done it. His successive acts were not blindly repeating what he had done so many times before. Each time he tried to see how the last time could be improved upon. The same holds good for the manager.

This does need some knowledge of principles and skills that can't always be discovered for one's self in the act of doing the work. Good management involves more than being familiar with the organisation you're working in and technically sound in the operations you're running — though anyone would be a fool to deny the importance of these things too. Indeed, they may take some time to acquire when a manager moves from one job to another or from one organisation to another. You can see this problem when industrial managers move into, say, local government. Until they've learned the ropes they're like landlubbers crewing a yacht, pulling all the wrong tackle and getting cracked over the head by the boom and generally making heavy weather of the whole exercise. But if they already think like managers — in other words, are familiar with the fundamental principles and skills involved in management — their inadequacies are usually only temporary. Habits of management thinking take longer to develop. They demand an understanding of what the principles and skills are that you are trying to put into practice. Without that understanding, it's only by accident that your experience teaches you how to be effective as a manager.

There is one thing that anyone does get from experience, and that is confidence in the way he's doing it — however bad his performance is. Practice doesn't make perfect, but it does a lot for the assurance of the guy who practises. And assurance has a nasty habit of turning into complacency and pig-headedness.

The cases that follow are factual, though details are disguised. All the managers are experienced in the sense that they have been managers for many years. The stories by themselves don't prove anything of course — they could be unfortunate incidents. But real managers wouldn't take that on trust. Yet there's no evidence that anyone at more senior levels in their organisations has seen any problem at all.

Try doing your own analysis of each one in the space below it: what is the management principle that is being flouted? At the end of the chapter we'll give you our idea so that you can compare it with your own.

1. Jack Crass is a technologist in a big company in the metals industry. For years he has been head of a technical problem-solving section that plays a vital role in tackling problems in production and in customers' applications of the products supplied. As a technical man he is brilliant. As a manager he is an incompetent bully who boasts of his power to reduce his subordinates to shivering jelly. Not surprisingly the technical abilities of his staff are mediocre — the more able people who are recruited do not stay long. But this does not completely explain their frequent failures to tackle technical problems successfully. Their over cautious approach and ingrained fear of using their own judgement is at least equally to blame. Crass himself is often unable to bring his own expertise to bear because of the time demanded by 'managing' his section.

Your analysis:

2. Tom Baile is a senior manager in a major public corporation. He had been given the responsibility for a multi-million-pound project that had been awarded to a large engineering contractor. Time deadlines were crucial to avoid high extra costs to the corporation. A planning meeting set up by Baile was attended by thirty corporation managers and technical staff plus five key men from the contractor. He ran this meeting as a single huge talking-shop in which corporation politics played as large a part as the need for the efficiency and economy of the plan. The contractor's planning meetings were run as working groups reporting back to a small controlling group: their side of the planning was completed within two weeks. After three months the corporation's plan was still incomplete because of key questions left undecided and vital points overlooked in the original meeting. The resulting delays caused to the project cost the corporation and the taxpayer several million pounds of unnecessary extra expense.

Your analysis:

---

3. Jimmy Howe was for many years in charge of the London advertisement sales department of a national group of local newspapers. The newspapers themselves operated in centres up and down the country. The sales department's business came from large London-based companies who placed advertisements for national sales campaigns throughout the group's newspapers. Despite this, the sales force was organised into teams that each sold advertisement space in only one centre's newspapers. For a customer company to arrange a national campaign involved visits from up to seven salesmen. The sales team-leaders tried for several years to get Howe to consider changing this organisational structure. They pointed out the waste of time for both salesmen and advertisers, and the frustration and poor morale in the sales force caused by the problems of coordination. All to no avail. The department was eventually closed down.

Your analysis:

4. Bill Myers is the manager of a large rubbish incinerator plant owned by a local authority. An essential part of the plant is its electrical equipment, which is maintained by some thirty electricians under the control of a supervisor. For some time there had been labour problems and threats of 'industrial action' in this group. The supervisor had done what was in his power to negotiate solutions but the situation was becoming critical. Several times he attempted to discuss it with Myers who seemed to regard the problems as trivial. He eventually succeeded in getting an appointment with him. After the supervisor had explained the background for a few minutes, Myers ended the meeting abruptly with a comment that he was not prepared to listen to his supervisor's problems because the supervisor never listened to his. Shortly afterwards, the men went on strike. The strike lasted for several weeks and was eventually ended by a concession from Myers — the very same concession that the supervisor had wanted to propose to Myers. He had been given no opportunity to discuss it during their meeting.

Your analysis:

5. George Turpin is Production Director of an engineering company employing about three thousand people. Most of them are employed in production and operate a fairly complex shift system. Manning rotas are drawn up by shop stewards who are quick to demand extra manning and overtime payments if there is the slightest variation in workshop schedules. On occasions, supervisors and managers try to resist the more unreasonable demands. However, they have learned that such efforts are often futile. Turpin will over-rule their decisions without reference to them when a steward insists on — and gets — a meeting with him. The effects on cost control are the despair of the Cost Accountant.

Your analysis:

---

6. Frank Aynsworth has been for many years the editor of a widely-circulated trade magazine, and is highly regarded throughout the trade for his ability as a journalist. His editorial department comprises about thirty journalists. His structure is uncoordinated, and private battles between section leaders are common because of loosely-defined and overlapping responsibilities. Editorial bright ideas are implemented with great enthusiasm but usually with too little persistence to achieve the results that would justify the effort expended on them. There is little effective control of editorial tasks apart from those that are Aynsworth's personal hobbies. For some time he has had a deputy who does have management ability (a somewhat rare quality in editorial departments). The deputy has tried to get some control over the department's problems but with little to show for it. Aynsworth refuses to give him the authority he needs on the grounds that he is not a good enough journalist.

Your analysis:

7. Bob Morris runs the central warehouse in a firm of builder's merchants. The company is organised into several areas, each controlling some six or seven branches. Each area is responsible for its own purchases of the materials and products sold through its branches. The area manager is judged by his area's profitability and has a free choice of sources of supply to find those that give him the best profit margins. The purpose of the central warehouse is bulk purchase and storage of goods for supply to the areas. This is, of course, to take advantage of bulk purchase discounts. The purpose makes sense, but Morris's costing policy for supplies to the areas removes half its point. He insists that the warehouse must show an artificial 10% net profit on everything it handles. This makes the warehouse charges for some goods higher than the prices external suppliers charge to the areas for their small-scale direct purchases. As a result, area managers use their own supply sources for many goods that would have greater profit margins for the Company if they were handled as bulk purchases through the warehouse.

Your analysis:

Did you see it this way?

1. Jack Crass
A typical example of a specialist who has been promoted into a management job. Possibly this is the only way his superiors can think of to reward his undoubted technical ability. They lack the organising skill to create higher level specialist roles that have equivalent status and pay to management roles but without the management responsibilities. Actually Crass is psychologically unfitted to have managerial authority over other people.

2. Tom Baile
A political player in a management job. Those over-large meetings give the game away. Typically the political player is the

person whose interests lie more in the direction of manipulating others than on getting things done efficiently — and a large group gives more scope for the manipulator than the small working party does. In footballing terms, he 'plays the other players, not the ball'. Perhaps it wasn't entirely Baile's fault. Organisational politics seemed to be a prime concern of most of his colleagues and superiors too. This was simply a rather worse mess than most of the others caused by these shenanigans.

3. Jimmy Howe
An example of the manager who can't see the relationship between the purpose of his operation and the way it's organised. His single priority was actually a financial one — to enable the costs and revenues produced by each sales team to be directly allocated to one or another of the newspapers themselves. Having developed a fixation with this idea, he simply ignored the damage it was causing to the efficiency of the work and the effectiveness of the people he was responsible for. Eventually the *financial* effects of these Work and People-type problems became too serious for his superiors to ignore. He failed to balance his priorities.

4. Bill Myers
The manager who doesn't understand what delegation means. He believes in a tit-for-tat theory of responsibility: 'if my subordinate isn't interested in helping me with my responsibilities, I won't help him with his'. Yah-boo and sucks to you. But the subordinate's responsibilities *are* his manager's responsibility. If the subordinate gives clear signals that he can't cope, the manager had better start thinking about the problem because now *his* responsibilities are at risk.

5. George Turpin
A sort of reverse kind of delegation problem — the manager who takes decisions when his subordinates have most of the practical information on which the decision ought to be based *and think they have the authority*. It's usually the sign of an inability to discipline himself to *maintain* his delegation. Given half a chance (e.g. a shop steward who insists on seeing the boss), the manager comes dashing in to re-take the decisions that his subordinates have already taken. This effectively pulls the rug from under their feet. How on earth can they earn any respect from their workforce for the authority they're supposed to have if the boss is constantly showing that *he's* not willing to support their authority?

6. Frank Aynsworth

Another version of the specialist's problem. The specialist who doesn't realise that the able manager of others in his special field often isn't a star performer himself. The good sales supervisor isn't usually a crack salesman. The best person to run the computer department isn't usually a computer genius. Certainly the manager needs enough knowledge of the specialism to recognise high performance and to understand what goes into achieving it. But his prime abilities lie in another direction.

7. Bob Morris

The manager who confuses entrepreneurial aims with those of management. He tries to run his part of the organisation as though it were an independent business. He operates on the profit–motivation theory, treating profit as the goal rather than as one of a number of yardsticks that should be used to measure the effectiveness of his management. In some organisations, it *is* possible to treat sub-units of the whole set-up as businesses in themselves — in which case the people who run those sub-units may need greater ability as businessmen than as managers. But you have to be able to recognise the bits you *can* do that with and the bits you *can't!* It didn't work in this case.

The experienced bad manager

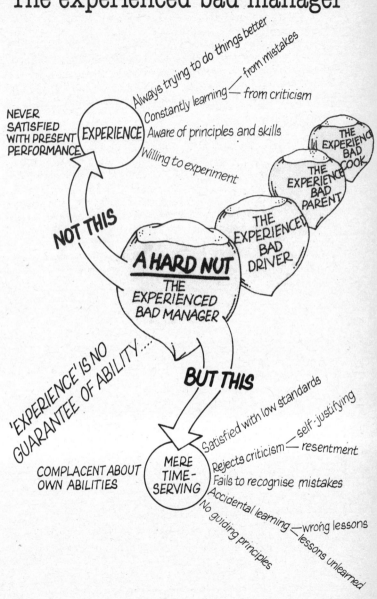

Always trying to do things better — from mistakes

Constantly learning — from criticism

Aware of principles and skills

Willing to experiment

NEVER SATISFIED WITH PRESENT PERFORMANCE

EXPERIENCE

THE EXPERIENCED BAD COOK

THE EXPERIENCED BAD PARENT

THE EXPERIENCED BAD DRIVER

NOT THIS

A HARD NUT
THE EXPERIENCED BAD MANAGER

'EXPERIENCE' IS NO GUARANTEE OF ABILITY...

BUT THIS

COMPLACENT ABOUT OWN ABILITIES

MERE TIME-SERVING

Satisfied with low standards

Rejects criticism — self-justifying

resentment

Fails to recognise mistakes

Accidental learning — wrong lessons

No guiding principles — lessons unlearned

10. Management skills

A manager's sense of his priorities is like a sense of balance, and like a good sense of balance it helps him to avoid stumbling. The Experienced Bad Manager is often like someone who has a faulty sense of balance, so he gets tripped more often. But there's obviously more to management than avoiding falling flat on your face. Any act of physical movement — walking, running, dancing, turning cartwheels — requires a sense of balance *and* skills of body control, even if it's only the skill of putting one foot in front of the other. So do the practical things that managers do. Any act of management involves skills that you can be aware of using and even do something to improve. The Experienced Bad Manager doesn't only have problems with his sense of priorities. He's also deficient in his skills of management action.

What are these skills? In 1955, Peter Drucker's famous book *The Practice of Management* was published. It was quickly recognised as a fundamental piece of work, a major step forward in understanding what good management involves. In one section of the book, Drucker sets out a list of what he called 'management operations'. He identified five of them, which are often shown diagramatically like this:

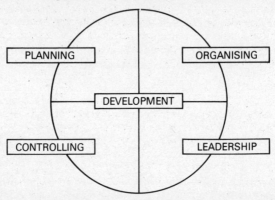

Whatever Drucker meant by his 'operations', most managers who know about them assume they are different activities. Now if this were true, a manager could say at one point in time 'I'm now planning' and at another 'I am now motivating my subordinates' and at another 'I am now organising something'. Which is nonsense if you think about it. Managers *can't* do these things as separate activities. So what are they? Could they be things the manager has to keep in mind as he manages — broad aims or concerns of different sorts? That's rather doubtful. These are the priorities we've already analysed: work, money and people.

Drucker himself talks about the abilities and skills needed to do the five operations. The point is that *they are themselves the skills* that enable the manager to perform his job. 'Planning' is a skill that's relevant to almost anything he does. So are 'organising' and 'controlling' and the rest. Drucker's achievement was to come up with a way of dividing the general ability to 'act like a manager' into its components. Just as the act of running involves several skills of muscle-control-movements of legs and arms, body posture, breathing and so on — any single act of management involves several of the five skills, and often all of them combined. Preparing for a new project uses your planning skills obviously, but also your skills in deciding the controls needed and in arranging the leadership of the people who'll be involved. A disciplinary interview tests your skills in motivation and communication (which are the words

Drucker uses for 'leadership'), but also your skills in controlling the problem and in planning the action that will follow.

In your job as a manager, you *use* the skills together. But if you want to *improve* your competence as a manager, you can identify the particular skill that needs improvement and work on it separately. And that's the real point of Drucker's masterly piece of analysis. It gives you the chance to be methodical about the way you identify your limitations and work on them.:

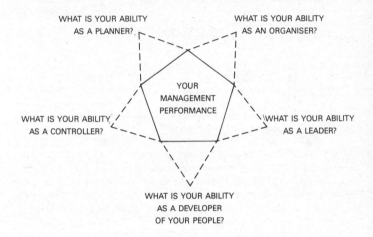

There's no particular sequence in the skills, so it doesn't particularly matter where we start. Convention puts planning first, so let's follow convention.

A. Planning

The skill of thinking ahead in deciding action.

The Experienced Bad Manager is often the manager who doesn't do it. He has a habit of leaping without looking. This can't be because he hasn't the ability to think about the future — every human being has enough imagination to do that. Maybe he's simply impatient, but he's also a bit short on the thinking skills of seeing the consequences of the decision he is making.

Foresight is involved, but it's more than that. Planning is the skill of applying foresight in your decisions about what's to be done next, and what next, and what next . . . as far forward as you can go in actually influencing the future course of events.

Not everything needs long-term planning, and you may be in no position to do it anyway. Some decisions don't require very high planning skills — for instance, working out a 'do-list' for the day or a number of points you want to attend to over the next week. Others don't give you the opportunity to use the skills to any great extent, like a quick decision on an urgent problem. The ones that do really test your skill is when you've got something big and long-term to prepare for — a project that will need several weeks to complete, say, or a major problem that will take more than a month or two to solve, or a budget for the next year. But although different activities need different *levels* of planning skill, they all involve the same *kinds* of skill.

Aim-setting: your skill in defining what you want to achieve whenever there is something to be done. A host of managers seem to tackle anything they've got to do simply as something to do. *Why* they're doing it is something they don't consider. They haven't developed the habit of thinking about the result they want, and their lack of the habit is often due to their lack of the skill of aim-setting. The only aim they can come up with is an aim to get it done, which doesn't get them any further forward. It also prevents a search for alternative lines of action.

Finding the right direction in which to move is a question of your skill in visualising the 'big picture' of what you're trying to do. The skill lies in thinking of the questions and knowing when you've found good answers:
- what's the point of doing it?
- is it practically possible to get that result?
- how will you know when it has been accomplished?
- how do you want to be placed at the end of it for whatever might happen afterwards?
- does your aim allow you to consider different ways of achieving it?

The test of your aim once you've got it sorted out is whether you're now able to take better decisions on alternatives and on the details of what's to be done. It's a poor aim that doesn't do this.

It's often more difficult to maintain an aim than to define it in the first place: when you're up to your backside in alligators, it's hard to remember your original intention was to drain the swamp. Many managers display almost a religious fervour about getting objectives established and then seem to forget all about them as soon as the action begins and problems begin to emerge. There's a skill in modifying and adjusting aims to suit actual circumstances, but it's no skill to forget them completely in coping with what comes up.

Understanding the problem: your skill in visualising in enough detail the differences between where you are now and where you should be by the time the action is over. 'Problem' is a negative word for this but it's hard to think of a better one that's as simple. It could be a problem, a difficulty of some sort you're tackling. Equally it could be something positive — a new development, an opportunity to achieve something. Whatever it is, there's a skill in mentally picturing the differences between the 'before' and 'after' situations, thinking about alternative routes you could take to get from one to the other, and searching over the whole picture for things that will need actions or decisions of some sort. It's easy to miss something vital if you don't do this. Given our natural interest in action and doing things, it's more likely to be something to do with costs and resources, or with people's involvement and attitudes, or with side-effects of the action you're planning.

This skill is one you don't exercise much if you're doing the same thing the same way you've done it a hundred times before. It's a recipe for disaster to take a manager without it, perhaps someone who has been running an unchanging operation for years, and ask him to set up a project that does need the skill — say a project to change the working arrangements and the organisation of the people in his area.

He'll blame the resulting mess on his lack of experience with such projects, but that isn't really the point. Another manager in the same situation may manage a similar project without trouble, simply because he *has* tried to understand the problem he's tackling.

If you've developed the skill, Murphy's Law is less likely to give you trouble: 'if a thing *can* go wrong, it *will*'. Your eye for detail will have revealed likely booby-traps so that you can include actions to defuse them. And if the plan you're responsible for suffers a derailment, you're just the sort of bloke to have a 'Plan B' up your sleeve — a contingency plan. But there's a snag. Other managers whose operations are regularly beset by the problems you've managed to avoid will attribute your success to luck, not skill.

Scheduling: your skill in dividing the doing of something into a succession of separate stages. A useful skill for a small-scale action like running an interview or a meeting, or planning a day's activities. Essential if the action is a big one like installing a new system or developing a team's abilities. Some managers seem to see any result they want others to achieve as involving a single 'lump' of activity. They don't have the mental skill of breaking it down into its component tasks and visualising their sequence to see where one task depends on another being completed. Without this skill, their estimates of timing and of the resources needed are so much guesswork. Their 'control' of the course of the events they have set in motion is either nonexistent, or it's done by sitting on the shoulders of their unfortunate subordinates and making instant decisions as the inevitable problems emerge. This is a frequent cause of the emergency decision-making that goes on in organisations.

Judging time: your skill in estimating how long it will take to get something done. Managers who lack this skill make their mistakes consistently in one direction: they always under-estimate the time needed — particularly when the actions they've decided on involve some sort of change or adjustment in people's abilities, attitudes or working relationships. Without realistic timings, a plan is guaranteed to collect problems like a cat collects fleas.

B. Organising

The skill of re-arranging resources to get things done more economically, with better coordination and control. Or the rearrangement may be needed because of a change in the tasks and activities to be performed. Part of the skill lies in seeing when you should reorganise something and when you shouldn't — when the confusion and demoralisation caused by changing things simply isn't worth the candle.

The trouble with the word 'organising' is that it gets mixed up with planning and controlling and personal temperament and several other qualities. Think of the way you picture someone if he's said to be 'well-organised'. Do you see someone who's decisive? Someone who's self-disciplined? Someone who gets on with things? Someone who seems to have a plan for whatever he does? If you think about it you'll see how confused the idea becomes.

But it's difficult to come up with a better word for the skills involved in making the best *total* use of the people and equipment and accommodation and materials and everything else a manager has under his control. Since they all cost money, and since money is the prime resource of the organisations that managers run, it all comes down in the end to making the best use of the money that's available. But although money is at the bottom of it, it's not a financial skill. Its results are economic, but the skill is more in seeing how one thing relates to another —

how one activity relates to another, how one group of people relates to another, how equipment relates to people, how resources relate to needs. Get the relationships right and you get economy.

Primarily it's concerned with the way managers arrange their people — the kinds of jobs their people have, the way the jobs are grouped into teams and sections and departments, the systems by which they collaborate and the work gets done. It's one of the skills a manager uses when he decides what to delegate (although that also tests his skills in leadership and control — and often his skill in developing his people). If he is skilful in organising his delegation, it enables him to use his own and his subordinates' time and abilities to better effect.

If a manager is a good organiser, the people who work for him have fewer problems of coordination. There will be less waste caused by their working at cross-purposes, fewer lapses caused by communication failures. Equipment and materials will be available when they're needed. People and things will be in the right place at the right time. In total, with a given amount of resources, his part of the organistion will get more done than parts that are run by poor organisers.

Generally the higher you go in an organisation the bigger is the scope you find for your organising abilities. A clerical supervisor may rarely have the opportunity to do more than reallocate the work of a few clerks or delegate a minor responsibility or adjust a system slightly. His range is limited. But a senior manager who's appointed to a job with fifteen functions reporting to him is going to need considerable organising skill when he decides how to reduce that number to manageable proportions. The Experienced Bad Manager often reveals his shortage of the skill in the job titles of people below him. Jobs like Coordinator and Progress-chaser could well be the inventions of managers who couldn't tell the difference between a scrum and a loose maul on the rugby field. Sometimes they conceal their organising failures by using titles like Deputy or Assistant for the dust-bin jobs they create, but that only sweeps the problem under the carpet.

The manager who sorts out the problem has the ability to combine the use of these skills:

Jobs: the skill involved in designing a job. If you've got it, the job's responsibilities and the abilities needed to do it can be clearly defined for whoever takes it on. If you haven't, the job will become what *his* interests and existing abilities make of it or what he feels pushed by circumstances into doing, not necessarily what *you* need to get done.

Structure: the skill involved in dividing a whole range of work into different jobs. It's a skill of being able to picture the activities in enough detail to see what has to be linked to what else, and to avoid the problem of responsibilities that float around in the organisation because they don't properly belong to anyone. It enables you to separate the entire activity into responsibilities that people can take on and areas that managers can manage without all of them getting their knickers in a twist over constant problems of coordination.

Systems: there's a skill in designing them so that they provide the coordination and controls that are needed without being too costly in the time and effort of those who'll have to operate them. There's also a skill in seeing where they're really needed and where they're superfluous. The manager who has systems for everything is often trying to use them to get done things that can really be achieved only by leadership ability.

C. Leadership

The skills of getting things done willingly and with good spirit by others.

Leadership is obviously much more than a question of skill. It depends partly on the attitudes of those who are led. In many industries, supervisors' leadership is illusory, not primarily because they lack the ability but because their workforces don't accept their leadership. A history of mismanagement and growing union power has made the shop steward the real leader on the shop floor. To make inroads on deep-seated habits of disbelief in management takes a supervisor with remarkable personal qualities of character, personality and determination. These aren't skills in the sense that you can develop them if you've a mind to. Nor is the basic characteristic that a leader needs of not feeling dependent on his subordinates' goodwill for his own self-confidence.

But there are skills in leadership too, skills that *can* be developed and *need* to be developed. Of all the abilities, leadership is the one that's most generally needed from top to bottom of the organisational hierarchy. At the lower levels, many managers can operate with limited planning and organising skills, but their lack of leadership skill is the one thing their organisations can least afford. The higher-level managers who appoint and direct them need the skill, not only to understand the qualities needed for leadership of the workforce, but also themselves to provide the leadership of their own management teams. Leadership is unlikely to develop at the bottom if it's absent at the top.

Take the Experienced Bad Manager whose failures are failures in this skill. Suppose for the moment they aren't caused by his personality or attitudes: he doesn't bully his people, nor is he weak with them; he gives them no direct cause to distrust his motives; he has enough strength of character to provide the leadership they need. *But he isn't doing so.* The casual attitudes and performance of his staff shows it. If you ask him about his people, about their interest in their work, about the strengths and limitations of their abilities, about their problems and ideas, he can't tell you. He gives you answers of a sort, but a small amount of probing shows he hasn't thought about such things in any depth. His people socialise but have no real feeling of pulling together as a team. *They'll* tell you about the things that frustrate them in their work but *he* can't. They complain of being kept in the dark and never knowing what's going on. Their morale is only so-so, discipline lax, but the work is getting done after a fashion and he can't see any problem. Do you recognise the picture?

All these straws in the wind show a problem of leadership skills:

Understanding people: it's not an attribute of someone's character. It's the skill of learning how people tick and understanding their temperaments and stages of mind: the skills used in listening to them, in reading the signals revealed by their behaviour, in understanding how they collectively influence each other. This isn't specialised stuff labelled 'Psychologists Only'. It's the kind of ability that gives a leader the sense of what scope he has to influence his people.

Motivating: there's a skill in knowing what you can do to influence your people's morale *positively* and what you should try to avoid. If you haven't got it you don't bother about their feelings — you just push them when necessary. If you have got it you know it takes time to build that kind of influence, but no time at all to destroy it. You'll know when and how to push, and when to hold off. You'll know that a lot of your effort has to be directed to reducing the sources of *de*-motivation that lie in bad organisation, lack of delegation, poor communication, weak discipline, uncertainty, injustice. The main incentive you can offer your people isn't likely to be financial. Motivation and good morale aren't built on money. They're built on the purpose and interest the work itself gives them. *Your* interest in *their* work and ability is the thing, pal, not your pep talks or your happy smiling face!

Team-building: this is your skill in getting your people to take an interest in sharing as a group their problems and the pressures on them. Leaders lead teams, not collections of individuals. Of course, how far you can go in creating team-sense is limited by the way your group is composed — the jobs as much as the people. Whoever decides its organisation needs skill in creating scope for that sense to develop. Good organisation isn't purely a question of efficiency. But given that there is the potential there, you yourself need skill in pulling the individuals together: skills in setting up work to require collaboration; skills in involving the group in decisions about aims, problems, methods of coordination — decisions that might generally be seen as yours alone to take.

Communicating: the practical skills of getting and giving information in ways that enlist people's interest and cooperation. The most important skill of all in leadership, and because *anyone* can talk, the most disregarded. The skill is in the way you put things, your manner, your sensitivity to reactions, your ability to listen with obvious interest. The different forms of communication each have their own variations on the basic theme. Writing needs greater imagination in thinking of what needs to be said without the promptings supplied in conversations. Meetings need stronger abilities in promoting team-work. Interviews need greater skill in building rapport.

These are the tactical skills of communication. There are also broader strategic skills in deciding when and how to communicate. If you have them, you don't use shop stewards to communicate management information to the workforce. You don't imagine you can get effective decisions from a meeting of thirty people. You don't wait until rumours start before putting your people in the picture.

D. Controlling

The skill of recognising whether you have a problem to tackle.

Of all the skills in management, this is the most widely misunderstood. The vast majority of managers use the word for the actions they take when something has clearly gone wrong, but that's not the skill of control. Their *actions* are governed by their skills in planning, organising and leadership. So they have no word for the skill used to know whether anything is going wrong and, if so, to understand why. Good control is a damn sight more skilful than seeing something happening and making an instant decision about it.

The skill is the one the manager uses in monitoring what is going on in his area — a skill that enables him to spot anything that's relevant to the decisions he might have to make. He can understand the significance of the information he's getting and can make good judgements about the need for action. This puts him in a better position to use his other abilities in any corrective action he takes himself. If the action isn't his to take, it enables him to give better information to whoever ought to be taking it — whether that's his boss or a subordinate. The skill is an essential one in delegating. The manager who's short on it is in a cleft stick over his relationship with his subordinates. Either he dumps responsibilities and authority on them, not knowing anything about their successes or failures until a disaster small or large lands back on his lap. Or he fusses them like a neurotic referee, interfering so much with their play that he's in danger of getting the ball-game he thought he'd delegated dumped back in his court.

Part of the skill is knowing what you're looking for — having a clear idea of what your people should be doing, the progress you're expecting in the work. Part of it is getting information about what their performance and progress actually is and making sense of it: before you start deciding anything, do you know *why* there's a difference between what you were expecting and what you actually see, and whether it's a problem? Three-quarters of the managers who are deficient in these skills have problems in their areas but don't know it. The other three-quarters are tackling problems that aren't problems. Which means that about half of them are doing both things at once: they're tackling the wrong problems.

So the skills of controlling are these:

Creating controls: there's a skill in setting up the controls you'll use to tell whether the work in your area is progressing as it should, whether its results are acceptable, and whether the resources you're responsible for are being properly used. Controls aren't the messages that tell you you've already got a disaster on your hands. If they're well-designed, they give you lead-time to act early before the problem has become real trouble. So this particular skill is one you use alongside your planning skills when you set up some action. You plan in the controls that will provide you with information on the course of the events you're about to set in motion: what will you need to know and when? This is also the skill that makes the difference between delegating and dumping — the skill you use in maintaining your subordinates' accountability for the way they use their freedom of action.

Supervising: a skill that's relevant to *every* level of management, not just to supervisors. Whether you develop it depends on your interest in knowing what is actually going on in the area of the organisation that you're responsible for. Many managers seem to think that the controls they've created (or that exist anyway) tell them all they need to know. But in fact the controls of reports and figures *cannot* do this, simply because when you set them up you cannot think of all the information you might need. Anyway, even if control systems could tell you all that, they would become far too complicated and expensive to operate. There's a skill in judging how much information you should design your controls to supply, and how much can be left to be gathered in your regular 'walkabouts' of your area and by your practical checks on how well it's working.

The skills of supervising are related to some of the skills of leadership, especially those of listening and reading signals. But supervising also involves being perceptive about the work that people are doing, and about the real or potential problems that the systems of figures and paperwork controls don't reveal. The manager who has this skill is imaginative about ways of finding out without becoming regarded as a snooper by his staff, or by any managers below him either. At the same time, he can rapidly spot any things that really deserve his management attention. The manager without the skill travels blind. The signs are there but he doesn't notice them.

Recognising problems: your skill in interpreting the information you're getting from your controls and your supervising. Strictly speaking all you get from either is *data,* not *information* — a mass of facts and details that don't signify anything until you've understood what's important about them. The skill is one of working out what they're actually telling you.

It's a skill of distinguishing between apparent problems and real ones. You may see something happening that ought not to be happening, but that doesn't always tell you *why* it has happened. Simply to know a problem exists may be enough to start emergency action, but often it's a failure of control that you have to take emergency action at all. Knowing reasons and causes is essential if you're to avoid being put in the position of a doctor whose answer for a case of measles is to try rubbing the spots away. A crop of machine breakdowns may be remedied by quick repair jobs without spotting the causes that lie in maintenance failures or lack of operator skill. Poor performance by staff may be answered by increased management pressure for results, while ignoring the real problems of their lack of ability in actually doing the work or of managers' own flabby leadership. If the cause isn't identified, the action will produce only temporary results and may make a bad situation worse.

The difficulty is that problems are usually revealed in the work but the problems themselves are something else. Problems with people and their management, with resources and their use, with the organisation's structure and its systems. To recognise the causes of work-problems that lie in people's attitudes, morale and abilities requires skills in understanding the people themselves: leadership skills have to be allied to supervising skills to unravel the knots. To see why a figure in a budget return is different from the figure it ought to have been and whether it points to a problem may require an understanding of the basis on which the budget has been set up: the planning skills involved in defining acceptable tolerances are as important as the skills of using financial control information. To understand the reasons for ineffective work and wasted time may call for a hard look at the way people's jobs are arranged: organising skills are needed to recognise the real underlying problem.

Part of the skill is noticing what *isn't*. Something that you might have expected to happen that didn't happen, like Sherlock Holmes's dog that *didn't* bark in the night. It might point to a problem that you'd otherwise miss. Or perhaps there's a problem that you'd normally expect but that didn't happen in the way you were expecting — it's there in a concealed form. A difficulty that someone *ought* to have had in doing something: when it doesn't arise, you're alerted and discover that there *is* a problem, but different from the one you'd imagined.

Another part of the skill is noticing effects that happen very slowly — a gradual deterioration in people's morale, a steady increase in a certain cost, an ominous rise in the incidence of some small problem. Unnoticed, these things can creep up on a manager unawares until suddenly he realises he has a major problem on his hands and it's too late to find an effective solution. To the manager who's skilled in controlling, small but persistent changes are things to be investigated before they get out of hand.

E. Development

The skill of managing the way people develop their abilities through experience.

Everyone knows that experience changes a person. Not his basic personality or character of course, but with experience he becomes more adept in his way of doing things and develops more confidence in his ability to handle situations. It's a process he's unconscious of, and for most of the time it moves slowly. Put into a new job, he'll learn a lot fairly quickly in the first few weeks and months, acquiring new knowledge and working habits. But after that his speed of learning slows down. It may appear to stop altogether after a few years in the job, but that's only because you can't see it happening. In fact it's still going on little by little, but it often isn't actually increasing his abilities any further. He may be learning how to conceal his difficulties better, how to make his job easier for himself or how to cope with its frustrations, but he's not necessarily becoming more competent at it.

The Experienced Bad Manager is himself an example of this process. Although he has been in management for years, he still isn't doing it terribly well, and further experience doesn't seem to develop the abilities he's missing. What's happening is a kind of double bind: the experience he's now getting is confirming the poor habits of thinking and behaviour he acquired, probably early in his management career. At the same time it's increasing his confidence in his way of doing things. His past experience is preventing him from using his present experience to develop further. It stops him from learning different approaches and new skills because they would mean changing old habits and trying unfamiliar ways of doing things. He becomes incapable of seeing any alternatives to what he is used to.

Many people, perhaps a majority, aren't getting full value out of the experience their jobs could offer them. Complacency severely limits the scope of some to go on improving their abilities. For others, it's lack of interest in what they're doing, or lack of the opportunity to take on tasks and problems that would stretch them. But for most, it's simply that they don't realise what there still is for them to learn. There are no criticisms of the way they're doing their jobs. They're getting results. So why bother?

It's a problem that the manager who's interested in his people's development is keenly aware of. His skill is a skill in making the self-satisfied a little more conscious of the things they could improve without demoralising them. It's a skill of building the nerve of the diffident to tackle things they don't believe themselves capable of. It's a skill of helping each and every subordinate to look at this job as something to continuously learn from, not simply something to do.

The good manager can encourage his subordinates to learn by experience, he can increase the amount they learn, but he can't hurry the process. It's the approach of the gardener to helping the growth of his plants, not the engineer's approach to a quick modification job on a machine. Think of the time it takes for anyone to develop the kinds of management skills we're analysing.

Or think of the time it takes for a newly-formed group to settle down and learn how to operate together. Even the eleven members of a football team need more than a match or two to get the hang of working together, and some teams don't manage it in a full season. In the days of the battleship it was reckoned to take at least a year for a crew of, say, a thousand to shake down and be ready for action. Cooperation and mutual understanding are among the things learned by experience, and they take time to develop even among staff whose managers realise what's involved.

But managers who are unskilled in development can *increase* the time it takes their people to learn by experience, can even cause them to learn the wrong lessons. Really poor management often concentrates people's minds on aspects of performance that don't help them to develop their abilities. That's the sort of management that continues to base payment systems on output rather than on effort when workers are learning how to operate new processes, pushing them to scramble through rather than build new skills. It's the sort of management that treats an individual's errors of judgement as disciplinary issues rather than opportunities for coaching, pushing him to avoid using his judgement rather than learn how to improve it. It's the sort of management that leaves a person new to a job to his own devices in trying to cope with unfamiliar work on the assumption that 'anyhow, he'll pick it up with experience'. Anyhow is often the way he does pick it up, acquiring poor attitudes to the work and making many more mistakes than is good for his job's efficiency or his own confidence.

Development isn't of course something the manager does to his subordinates. It's a collaborative exercise. He needs the skill in the first place to recognise the scope to improve something in their abilities. But that's not enough — he also needs the skill to enlist their interest in making the improvement happen. They have to do the learning. He can't do it for them. And if they know what it is they can usefully learn, they're more likely to get those lessons out of their experience. So the skills are all skills of sharing ideas with your subordinates on how their performance and their abilities can be improved:

Standards of performance: your skill in defining the quality of performance you expect from your people. The manager who lacks this skill makes one of two mistakes. Either he accepts mediocre performance as a norm from his people — a level of quality below the level they are actually capable of achieving — or he expects the impossible. Having high standards isn't a skill in itself of course. The skill is in knowing whether the standards you are getting from your subordinates are high standards for them, and where they could be improved.

There's an important point here. The standards are standards of *performance,* not necessarily of *results.* Developing people isn't just a question of putting pressure on them to get better results and expecting them to improve their abilities of their own accord. Poor results may not be the fault of people's performance — they may be due more to the situations they are trying to cope with or to their managers' own failures of management. An able person given a difficult task may produce a result well below his previous achievements, but that's not the thing you're trying to measure. The real question is 'how well is he handling it compared with the way someone of less ability would handle it?' The skill is one of knowing how to compare the quality of different people's performance in similar tasks, and how to recognise improvements in someone's performance that come from improvements in his ability. No improvement at all is needed to get better results out of an improving situation, but improvement really is demonstrated if results are maintained when the situation is getting worse.

Recognising what can be learned: your skill in distinguishing between abilities that can be developed and those that can't. Many managers can't spot the difference. Some persist in trying to work personality changes in their subordinates. Others take the inevitable failure of such attempts as general proof that abilities can't be developed: 'either you've got it or you haven't' they'll say. They miss the point that facets of anyone's temperament and character — facets that may well affect his performance in a job he's doing — are indeed fixed, but that a wide range of knowledge and skills that would enable him to perform better can be learned. The development skill is one of identifying the *learnable* knowledge and skills that could improve his performance.

Appraising: your skill in judging people's capacities to improve their abilities. It's a skill of reading each person's strengths and — what is more difficult — his potential strengths, and of recognising his limitations that have to be accepted. An ability he needs may be one that *can* be developed. But the scope for him as an individual to become highly competent in that particular direction may be limited by the sort of person he is. For instance, the skills of writing reports are learnable skills. But an engineer or salesman whose extravert outgoing temperament makes him impatient with paperwork may find it difficult to acquire those skills to any high degree. Or take the management skill of understanding other's attitudes and states of mind. It *can* be learned, but a manager who is self-centred or insecure by nature may be hard put to develop more than a rudimentary ability in reading the signals of apathy and poor morale among his staff. If you're skilled in appraising to recognise such limitations, you don't necessarily give up hope of any improvement at all. But neither do you expect to achieve any radical transformations. In any case, it would hardly be surprising even when you're skilled if you occasionally misread people's capacities to develop abilities that may be non-existent at the moment. The most unlikely person can sometimes develop — or reveal — an ability that no one thought him capable of.

The manager practices this skill obviously enough in that once-a-year (or whenever) activity that goes by the name of 'Staff Appraisal'. But that isn't the only occasion for it. Developing his subordinates is a year-round occupation for him, and he constantly has opportunities to adjust and refine his judgements of their actual and potential capacities. Remember it's a skill, not an activity, and the more often the skill is exercised the more it is developed.

The skill is a vital one in selecting someone for a job or in making decisions about his promotion or transfer from one job to another. You should be able to discover whether his experience has got him to the starting line — whether it has given him the basic abilities to take on the job. But you also have to ask yourself whether he has the personal qualities and the calibre and intelligence to learn the further abilities needed to make a success of it. Can you see the potential in him to develop them once he's in the job? The skill lies in neither appointing a candidate whose personal qualities are unsuited to the job, nor rejecting out of hand a candidate who's a bit limited in abilities that he is perfectly capable of acquiring with a few months' experience.

Creating opportunities: your skill in finding ways for your people to develop their abilities through the experience they get in their jobs. Some managers have a great deal of skill in seeing opportunities for development in situations where other managers would see no scope. They'll take a regular feature of a subordinate's job that others would take for granted, and say: 'Now let's look at this to see what can be learned from it. How do you do it at the moment? Why do you do it that way? What kinds of problem do you get in doing it? What's the knowledge or skill you're actually using? What further knowledge or skill would help you do it better? Let's work out a plan for you to develop that over the next few months . . .' Even in a run-of-the-mill operation, they have the knack of spotting the ways they can use their people's work to give them coaching.

A lot of the skill of creating opportunities for development is in seeing the scope for it that is there already in people's day-to-day activities. If you have good, clear standards of performance, there should be no difficulty in identifying for each of your people *which* of his abilities could be further developed. The question is *how* . The first direction in which you look is to help him turn some part of the work he's doing into an exercise to develop that ability.

Some opportunities come ready-made — the problems and difficulties that people are already aware of, but often see as problems caused *for* them rather than *by* them. The manager who is skilled in development can take the problems that his people have created for themselves, perhaps without realising it, and use them as launch-pads for development: 'How did that problem come about? Was that the real problem? Where did it actually begin? Suppose you had the situation to deal with again, is there anything you could do differently? What kind of approach could you develop for the future? . . .' One of the biggest difficulties in development is to make people aware that something better is needed. A problem that someone is aware of in his work is a major step towards getting him to see where his own abilities could be extended.

But apart from the opportunities that already exist, the manager can create others that stretch his people's knowledge and abilities. He can deliberately allocate tasks a little beyond his subordinate's present experience. He can involve his people in investigating regular problems in his area. Most important of all, he can increase their freedom of action to control things for themselves — in other words he can delegate more fully.

The skills of management are often called 'mere' commonsense, as though anyone with a bit of nous has them anyway and they don't need to be developed. If that were true, the Experienced Bad Managers in our organisations would have cornered the market in stupidity. The fact is, most of them are pretty intelligent individuals, but they are all short on these skills in one way or another. Perhaps this goes to show what a rare sense 'common-sense' is.

The point of seeing an ability as a skill is to look on it as something that you can learn. *All* these skills are learnable. It's a question of applying whatever development skill you already have to your *own* self-improvement as a manager.

Management skills

PLANNING
- Aim-setting
- Scheduling the tasks
- Judging time
- Understanding the scope of what you want to get done

THINKING AHEAD

ORGANISING
- Defining jobs - allocating work
- Structuring their relationships
- Designing systems of work

ARRANGING RESOURCES

MANAGEMENT SKILLS

MAINTAINING MORALE

LEADERSHIP
- Understanding people
- Understanding how to influence their MOTIVATION
- Team-building
- Communicating-reading signals

MAKING IMPROVEMENTS

DEVELOPMENT
- Creating opportunities for learning
- Setting standards of performance
- Recognising what can be learned
- Appraising people's capacities to improve

KNOWING WHAT'S GOING ON

CONTROLLING
- Creating controls
- Supervising
- Recognising problems

11. Blocks in thinking

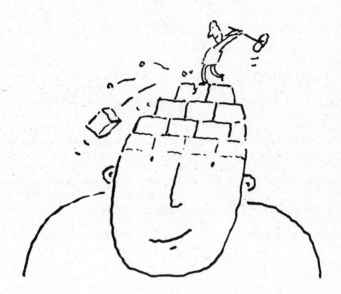

A lot of the job of any manager is active — talking to people, dealing with one thing after another, showing others what they have to do, coping with practical problems. But also a lot of his work is thinking. If his thinking is poor, a great deal of his activity will be misdirected. Most of the management skills we've been looking at involve using one's brain-power more effectively.

Busy, practical managers often under-rate the thinking side of their jobs. The qualities they reckon they need include drive and energy, yes. Decisiveness, yes. Commonsense, yes. But the ability to think? That's something for professional people, academics, writers and others who live by their brains. Managers are too occupied coping with actual events and real problems to play intellectual exercises. And that's many people's view of what 'thinking' means. It's something that's clever to do and a bit mysterious.

In fact thinking is so ordinary that we do it without realising that that is what we're doing. It's what fills the time between waking and sleeping, except when routines or emotions take control. Thinking is what you do when the car won't start — after you've finished swearing. It's what you do when you've got three things to do and time only to do one of them. It's what you do when you're trying to understand a complicated explanation. It comes into every problem you tackle, every decision you take. Perhaps your thinking isn't terribly good in some cases, but you can't avoid doing it somehow.

In this sense managers *do* need the ability to think, though they might call it 'using common-sense'. It's the ability to size up situations, solve problems, decide actions. Their problems are practical, their decisions are practical, so their thinking has to be practical too: 'what's really happening here?' 'why is it happening?' 'what could it lead to?' 'what ought to be happening?' 'what should I do about it?' The questions may be different from those that concern the academic or intellectual kind of thinker, but the processes going on in their minds are very similar.

Anyone *can* improve his thinking ability if he sets about it the right way, but most of us don't make the attempt. Perhaps we have never considered the possibility, in the same way that it doesn't occur to most people to do anything about other basic activities like the way they breathe or walk or talk. Perhaps we are quite satisfied with the way we do it already and don't see any need to change. Even if we'd like to be better at thinking, we are put off by two very powerful ideas. Both happen to be wrong.

The first is the idea that a person's ability to think is governed by his intelligence. If you believe this and happen to be intelligent, it will be hard to persuade you that you *need* to learn anything about thinking. By the same token, if you're less intelligent you'll assume that you *can't* learn to think any better. Your quota of brain-power is fixed, you'll reckon, and there's nothing you can do to increase it.

The error lies in confusing brain-power and thinking. Many intelligent people don't use their intelligence very effectively. People with less actual intelligence can sometimes be better at using the brain-power they've got. To say that your thinking ability depends on your intelligence is the same as saying that your driving skill depends on the horsepower of your car. A skilled driver may make better use of a Mini than a poor driver makes of a Ferrari. Better the Mini driver who completes his journey safely and in good time than the Ferrari driver who takes short cuts that turn out to be not so short and drives too fast for his own driving ability and winds up at the wrong destination.

And that's what is often done by highly intelligent people who are not good thinkers.

The second false idea is that a person's thinking ability has to do with his level of education. Highly educated people usually know a lot, though their knowledge may be in a very narrow field. But often they are surprisingly bad at thinking. Some of the best educated people with university degrees and doctorates can make a mess of thinking out quite a simple practical problem. You might say they're too clever and see all sorts of complications that don't really exist, but that's just poor thinking. It's really the fault of an educational system that pumps a lot of knowledge into them so that they can pass exams but teaches them little about how to use their brains, which is what thinking actually means.

In fact if someone does know a lot about a subject, it can stop him thinking out his own answers to questions about it — he just produces the stock answers he has learned. Not that it's wrong to be knowledgeable. You need knowledge of a subject to be able to think about it. But remembering what you already know isn't really thinking. Thinking is *using* your knowledge to work out your own answer to a problem that has just cropped up.

In the problem-solving and decision-making they do, managers are more likely to rely on their experience than their education. It's true that the kind of knowledge you get from experience is different from the kind you get from books and schools and training courses. For management it's often more valuable because it's knowledge of how you've been able to handle real-life situations and problems. But again it's mainly knowledge that experience teaches you. It doesn't necessarily teach you how to think out a situation you haven't met before or to develop a new approach to an old problem. In fact it's quite likely to dissuade you from searching for new approaches. If you imagine that experience is all you need to answer the questions you should be dealing with as a manager, it has much the same sort of snags as book-learning.

Managers need thinking ability as well as knowledge and experience and reasonable intelligence. And thinking is something anyone can learn to do better. The first thing is to recognise what might prevent you from using your brain-power as effectively as you might.

There are three major difficulties that reduce the ability to think clearly:

— ego-defence
— tramlining
— black boxes

Ego-defence

The ego is what the psychologists call a person's idea of himself. It's his idea of the sort of person he really is — which may be slightly different from the way other people see him and from the actual person himself. How this idea is formed is a complicated business to do with his background and upbringing that we needn't go into here. The point is that the idea is vitally important to him. It's not a matter of what he *wants* to believe about himself. It's what he's *got* to believe about himself if he is to maintain a sense of personal worth.

Each of us is prepared to spend quite a lot of emotional energy protecting our ego, particularly when we get into situations that make it difficult. A manager for instance may see himself as strong, self-reliant and able to control the situations he finds himself in. But many of those situations may actually be a bit beyond his capabilities alone, so he has to make an effort to maintain his view of himself and perhaps needs to indulge in small pieces of self-deception. The result may be the kind of behaviour that other people see as pig-headed or self-important. This is what ego-defence means. It is a pattern of feelings and behaviour by which each of us maintains his private concept of himself.

Quite a lot depends on how central a particular idea is to one's ego. Not everything a person believes about himself is equally important to him. In fact the same idea may have different weights in different people's egos. To one person the idea that he looks personally presentable may be very important; another person whose ego depends more on a sense of being sympathetic and kindly, say, many not be much concerned at all about his own appearance. The more central an idea is to a person's ego and the more easily it's threatened, the more active his ego-defences will be in protecting it.

Some people seem to need to make few efforts to maintain their belief in themselves. They are at ease with themselves and with others. Perhaps the things that are central to their egos are easier for them to maintain, less likely to be put under strain by the actual circumstances in which they operate. Perhaps they have a more realistic idea of themselves. They know their own strengths, accept their limitations and so don't need strong ego-defences. Other people seem constantly to be striving to buttress their egos. The person who is self-conscious, who is sensitive to personal indignities, who takes superior attitudes to others as a way of convincing himself that he matters is simply trying to maintain his central beliefs about himself. The same goes for the person who avoids difficult situations, necessary confrontations, tasks where he might risk failure. These too are ego-defences.

The trouble is that the mind that's engaged in defending itself can't think rationally about situations in the world outside, can't even see those situations clearly for what they are. Thinking clearly means looking at situations *objectively*. But whenever a person's ego-defences are active, his thinking is inevitably *subjective*. The way he looks at each situation he is involved in is distorted because he subconsciously homes in on those factors in it that are important to his ego. This means that he can often fail to recognise other important factors, simply because his thinking is being diverted. Even if he does notice them, they still don't get proper attention in his thinking.

Arrogance is an ego-defence — the insistence on *always having to be right*. And arrogance does more to hamper the ability to think clearly than almost any other personal attribute. People who pride themselves on their intelligence or status can be more arrogant than most. The arrogant intelligent person can find a good argument for the rightness of his point of view however wrong or misguided it may be in real terms. His quick mind enables him to reach an adequate solution to a problem on very little evidence. Having done so he'll ignore further evidence that would have enabled him to find a better solution, because that would mean accepting that his first idea wasn't so good after all. Because it supports his feelings of superiority he finds it more satisfying to criticise other people's ideas rather than constructively develop them into a workable form. Often he makes mistakes in his thinking because he's proud of his ability to find answers quickly. He simply thinks too fast.

The arrogance of status can bring different problems in its train, and it isn't restricted to senior management. A supervisor whose main concern is to maintain his feelings of superiority over his work-force can suffer from it as much as a director. The status-conscious person is likely to reject lower-status people's views because of their source, not because there's any rational argument against them. In conversations with others he will often listen too little and talk too much — status is maintained by holding the floor. So he misses a lot of the information on which his thinking ought to be based. He too finds it satisfying to demolish other's ideas but more often on the basis of his experience or the private information his status gives him access to, rather than by criticising the ideas directly: '*I* can tell you it won't work' he says, but won't risk an explanation of his reasoning that might reveal flaws in it.

Most of these kinds of problems are avoided by the person

who has built into his picture of himself a further idea — 'I am a thinker'. If you see yourself as a good thinker, you become proud of your ability to use your mind to explore a subject, to understand what is actually happening in a situation, to see possibilities and think through their consequences. It is easier to maintain an idea of yourself as a thinker than an idea that depends on your always being right.

Tramlining

'Genevieve' was a comedy film about a race between two veteran cars from London to Brighton and back. If you've seen it you'll remember the ending. Kenneth More as one of the drivers is in the lead approaching the finish of the race, but his wheels improbaby get trapped in some old tramlines in the roadway that lead him helplessly off in the wrong direction. Tramlines in the brain capture our thinking in the same way, though we're not usually conscious of their effects.

The tramlines are mental habits — the unquestioning acceptance of familiar ideas, set angles of approach to familiar problems, fixed attitudes to familiar people, regular ways of thinking about familiar situations. They are ruts in our thinking that are dug by experience of seeing the same situation again and again, going through the same thinking process time after time, doing the same thing over and over. Not only individuals but whole organisations tramline along in ways that are often ineffective and wasteful. Letters and reports are written in a ponderous, impersonal style that owes more to tradition than to clarity and conciseness.

Budgets prepared on the time-honoured basis of 'adding a bit to last year's figures' become justifications for unnecessary spending rather than guides to economy. Managers fixated by convential notions of 'managerial authority' behave towards their subordinates in ways that could hardly do more to reduce morale and commitment. Problems are allowed to persist simply because people are used to dealing with them.

Despite this, tramlining does have its value. Like the ability to tie your tie without thinking how you're doing it, it's useful — even necessary — for routine activities that don't need thinking out afresh each time. It allows you to run such things on automatic pilot, leaving your brain-power free to concentrate on other things that do need thinking about. It's like driving a car. The inexperienced driver has to think so hard about his use of accelerator, brakes, clutch and gear-lever that he can't cope with difficult situations in actually driving the car. The experienced driver has turned the way he operates the controls into tramlines in his mind. Gear-changing, braking and the rest are almost automatic actions for him, and he can concentrate his conscious thinking on his steering, speed and what's happening in the road ahead.

But tramlining is a positive menace when thinking really needs to be done. The motorway driver who lets his mental tramlines take control of his driving while he daydreams or chats with his passengers isn't thinking what he's doing. His mind is no longer trying to read traffic situations correctly, isn't on the lookout for potential hazards that require positive decisions about his course and speed. Similarly for the manager. The mental tramlines laid down through years of experience can trap his thinking when he ought to be aware of changing situations, new possibilities, different dangers. They stop him questioning his standard way of dealing with a problem or even looking for further information about it beyond what he knows already. The rails run straight from something he has observed to what he assumes the problem to be and on to a solution that's already prepared in his mind. He sees staff idle, assumes they are being lazy, and promptly gives them a rocket (or whatever his tramline solution is). He sees costs rising, assumes money is being wasted, and launches a blanket restriction on spending. And the reverse: busy staff, no problem, no action — though their work may be poor quality or involve a lot of wasted effort. Costs within budget, no problem, no action — though a lot of the spending may be uneconomic.

Managers aren't the only people who get trapped in tramline thinking like this, not by a long chalk. But it can do more damage when a manager gets stuck in inappropriate mental tramlines than when most other people do, because of the importance of the decisions he makes and his power to misdirect the thinking abilities of others.

Often the reason is that he is accepting a conventional idea without asking himself whether it's valid: 'Administrative work is all red tape'. 'Budgets are the province of accountants'. 'People generally need to be told what to do'. 'Manual labour is unskilled work'. 'Women can't cope with managerial responsibility'. 'Training isn't a manager's job'. 'Theories are useless in practice' . . . and all the other notions. Most of them wouldn't emerge unscathed from just five minutes clear, well-informed thinking about them, but it's surprising how many managers seem to take them as gospel truth.

Often it's a failure to be observant. The manager may treat one situation as exactly the same as others he's dealt with before, and fail to notice something different in it this time. So he tramlines his way to a decision rather than looking for the cause. An increase in wastage is treated as a production problem; he doesn't connect it with the lower quality material that a new and 'cheaper' supplier is providing. A fall in output is put down to lack of effort by staff; he doesn't trouble to find out about a major difficulty they had to exert themselves to overcome.

A very common reason for tramline thinking is the comfort and security it seems to offer. The manager who assumes that his experience tells him everything he needs to know about a situation spares himself from worrying about what he might be missing. The familiarity of the tramlines give him the feeling that he is doing the correct thing. If he is under stress he may need the reassurance they give him. Someone who is anxious or feels pressured may find it almost impossible to break free from his stereotyped approach to look around for angles he hasn't considered before.

There is yet another reason for tramlining. The manager may have inadequate knowledge of whatever he is dealing with. He works out an approach based on half-understood principles and simplistic ideas about the subject, a 'safe' approach that keeps him out of trouble. And that's the approach he sticks to whenever he has to tackle a question on the subject. This is the 'black box' problem

Black boxes

In thinking, a black box is anything that concerns you but that you don't really understand. The TV set at home is a good example. It's a very familiar object to you, but if you're like most people you've got only a vague idea how it actually works. Your knowledge is limited to the way you have to operate the controls to get the output you want — the picture. If it develops a fault you're sunk without a repair-man handy. You wouldn't have a clue about how to put it right, or even to find out what's wrong.

Fortunately there are plenty of repair-men about if your TV set goes wrong. So the only problem for you to think out is how to arrange a time for him to call when someone will be in. But suppose there were no such people as TV repair men. Or suppose they could do a repair only when you had diagnosed the fault. That's the real problem with black boxes in your thinking — the problem of having to think about something you don't fully understand when you are the only person who can do the thinking.

Most of the black boxes in a manager's thinking are not highly technical or scientific. He doesn't actually need to understand the internal mechanism of computers or production machines or office equipment because he doesn't have to make decisions about it. In fact, few of his black boxes are physical objects at all. They're nearly all *systems* of one sort or another that he *does* need to be able to think about. For instance, different managers might have a black box problem with one or more of these:

- a computer system a manager is involved with. If he doesn't understand it he can't think to much purpose about any problems the system creates for him, about what he would like it to do for him, about what it's not doing that it could be doing. No point in saying that these things are for the systems designers to work out. Unless he understands what the system is and isn't capable of, he can't communicate with the systems designers to work out the best solutions from both *his* point of view and *theirs*.

- how money behaves in his organisation. If he doesn't understand the way his operation's costs are made up, how the budgetary controls operate, what cash-flow means and so on, he can't think clearly about the economy of his operation. The accountants can't do this kind of managerial thinking for him. It has got to be done by the person who makes the practical operating decisions, and that's *him*.

- the operations of other parts of the organisation that his own operation links with. If he doesn't understand them, he can't work out with their managers good answers to problems of coordination. He has to know what *they're* trying to do (and perhaps what they *ought* to be trying to do) if he's to join with them in finding solutions that satisfy both sides. And the same applies to another common black box in a manager's thinking — the way his employees' union operates.

- the way managers at higher levels operate. If he doesn't know, he can't think constructively about the information he is passing on to them and the way he is presenting it. Nor can he interpret the instructions he gets from above into effective decisions for his own operation.

- what goes on at lower levels. When managers at the middle or senior levels treat this as something they don't need to understand for their decision-making, they run the risk of making foolish, even unworkable decisions on practical operational matters. Nor can they think clearly and realistically about their delegation to lower levels.

- people. For the manager who is uninterested in people as people, their attitudes and motivations are black boxes in his thinking. If he doesn't understand them as individuals and how they operate together, his thinking about their morale and effort is almost certain to be unrealistic. His judgements about their abilities are likely to be wrong. His attempts to persuade are doomed to failure. As a manager he is constantly acting at a huge disadvantage.

Managers who suffer from the black box problem with things like these may actually not be aware of it as a problem. But it is difficult if not impossible for them to apply their thinking abilities *effectively* to questions about them.

The manager who lets something that concerns his operation remain as a black box in this thinking reveals the problem in different ways. Often he won't realise if anything is wrong with it because he doesn't understand what ought to be happening. Without an understanding of his people he won't know the state of their morale or whether it could be better than it is. Without an understanding of costs, he won't know whether he has a problem with them or even how his decisions affect them.

Even if he does suspect there's a problem, he can't tackle it effectively. He may often misunderstand what it is. If he tries to deal with it himself, his ideas on how to deal with it are going to be inappropriate and naïve. He may often make a bad situation worse, like someone who tries to repair a major malfunction in his TV set and ends up causing greater damage than the original fault. Alternatively he calls in an expert for a minor adjustment that he could well have done himself. Accountants, personnel people, equipment specialists, industrial relations executives find themselves asked to tell him what to do when he's the person who ought to be making the decision. He excuses himself from the responsibility with phrases like 'it's not really my field' or 'I'm not supposed to know about that'.

Black boxes are not locked except by bad management conventions. The manager *can* get inside them if he puts his mind to it. In any case, he doesn't usually need the detailed knowledge of the expert, but rather a good practical sense of how the thing works and what it's possible to do. If there's a problem it's often enough to understand it and to know whether it's one he can handle himself.

Blocks in thinking

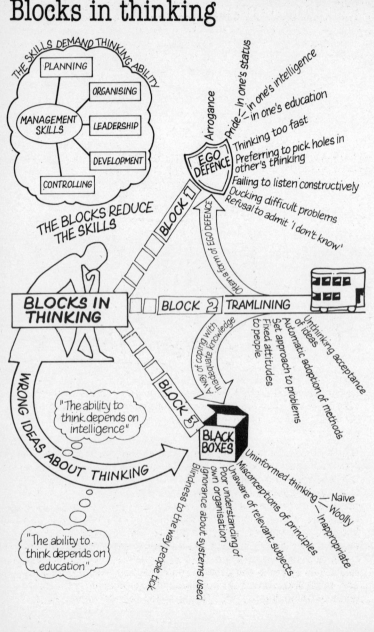

THE SKILLS DEMAND THINKING ABILITY

PLANNING

ORGANISING

MANAGEMENT SKILLS

LEADERSHIP

DEVELOPMENT

CONTROLLING

THE BLOCKS REDUCE THE SKILLS

BLOCKS IN THINKING

WRONG IDEAS ABOUT THINKING

"The ability to think depends on intelligence"

"The ability to think depends on education"

BLOCK 1

Arrogance

EGO DEFENCE

Pride – In one's status
– in one's intelligence
– in one's education

Thinking too fast

Preferring to pick holes in other's thinking

Failing to listen constructively

Ducking difficult problems

Refusal to admit 'I don't know'

Often a form of EGO DEFENCE

BLOCK 2 TRAMLINING

Unthinking acceptance of ideas
Automatic adoption of methods
Set approach to problems
Fixed attitudes to people

A way of coping with inadequate knowledge

BLOCK 3

BLACK BOXES

Uninformed thinking — Naive
Misconceptions of principles — Woolly
Unaware of relevant subjects — Inappropriate
Poor understanding of own organisation
Ignorance about systems used
Blindness to the way people tick

12. Improving your thinking

As a manager, there are two main things you can do to develop your ability at thinking. Neither of them is terribly difficult. But both do need a certain attitude plus some mental effort and persistence.

A. The first is to recapture some of that curiosity we all had as children. The curiosity to know WHY things happen and HOW things work. What defeats us so often as adults is that we get too used to a world in which we simply accept things for what they are — or more accurately for what we suppose them to be. Often we assume we *do* understand, when in fact our knowledge is very shaky and may actually be wrong. If we're aware of our lack of knowledge, we're too ready to assume we *can't* understand (perhaps through weak self-confidence or reluctance to make the effort), too ready to cover up our poor understanding with a bold front (usually because of natural pride and fear of looking foolish). The first step to better knowledge is the willingness to say 'I don't know' and 'I'll make it my business to find out'.

B. The second thing is to regard thinking as a *skill*. If you do this, you put it in the same category as cookery, piano-playing, car-driving, map-reading, playing darts, football and so on — an ability you can learn to improve. Like these other abilities, some people will always be able to do it better than others. But anyone can improve his ability at it if he has the will to make the effort. The desire to become more skilled is the starting-point. After that, the knowledge of what it involves and persistent practice in using the skills on the day-to-day problems, questions and needs that arise in one's management job.

A. The ladder of knowledge

Suppose there is a problem that you as a manager ought to be tackling, a problem that requires you to have knowledge of a certain kind to tackle it successfully. Let's say for the sake of the argument that it's a problem of future labour costs in the area you control. You have to understand the nature of the problem to work out a good solution to it. The knowledge you need is of a particular method of labour costing and evaluation that your organisation uses.

Let's say that you can't assume the accountants will work out the problem for themselves. In the first place they don't yet know there's a problem — you're the only person in a position to foresee it. Even if they did know about it, it's important that the solution isn't based simply on narrow accountancy criteria. It also has to take account of operational needs that you're responsible for satisfying.

Your ability to tackle the problem successfully depends on where you are standing on a ladder of knowledge about the labour costing method. it's a ladder with its rungs at five levels:

Level 1: Ignorance
You don't know the knowledge exists. You are totally unaware of the fact that your organisation has any particular labour costing method. If you knew, you could find out about it. But since you're completely in the dark, you can't start asking about it.

This is not an unusual situation for managers who limit their interest in their work to matters of immediate practical concern. The knowledge they're blind to may actually be to do with things that are very familiar to them. It's like the object in a hide-and-seek game that's 'hidden' by putting it in a very obvious place — so obvious that no one sees it as what they're looking for. It's often difficult for managers to make themselves aware of what they don't know about familiar situations. For instance they may be constantly conducting staff interviews without the slightest idea that there is a body of interviewing techniques and skills that they could learn to advantage. They may not realise they have anything to learn about the psychology of the groups of people they are regularly working with. It may never have occurred to them that the time-shortages they are always suffering from are directly due to their own ignorance of planning methods.

To become aware of what *might* be useful to know as a manager, you have to spread your net of interest widely. You have to be ready to pick up hints and ideas in talking with people inside and outside the organisation. It helps too to have an appetite for wide-ranging reading. The good manager is a generalist in his range of interests as well as his range of activities.

Level 2: Awareness
You know the knowledge exists, but not what it is. You've heard about your organisation's method of labour costing, but you don't know much about it. Lacking that knowledge, you don't realise you've got a problem — and without realsing that, you've no particular reason to try to get the knowledge. It may not appear to be relevant to you.

In management jobs, it's usually easy to find reasons for *not* trying to get proper knowledge of things that managers are aware of but don't really know. There isn't time. There isn't any way to get the knowledge. It's not their business to know it. There wouldn't be any point in their getting it. But often you have to get the knowledge before you can see its real value.

Level 3: Simple knowledge
You know the knowledge but can't use it. You know how the labour costing method is supposed to work because the accountants have explained it to you in detail. You may think you know enough. But actually you can't properly connect this knowledge with the practical problem that you're faced with. You might know enough to be aware you've got a problem, but not enough to understand the real nature of the problem or to see how best to tackle it. Your knowledge is too narrow or theoretical — though you probably don't realise this. You are at the risk summed up in the line 'A little knowledge is a dangerous thing'.

This is the situation in which a lot of education and training leaves its students. They are filled to the gills with booklore but can't apply it in the real world. It is the problem of schoolchildren whose maths lessons have left them incapable of doing a simple household budget. It is the problem of college students whose English classes have failed to teach them how to set down a logical written report. It is the problem of managers who've attended courses on industrial psychology but who cannot use what they have learned to get any better understanding of their own people. Knowledge is treated as something that's valuable for its own sake rather than something whose value is in its *use*.

There is a similar situation for the manager who receives a lot of facts and figures that are supposed to tell him what is going on but that he actually can't interpret. It's the sort of stuff that's often called 'management information' but more properly ought to be called 'data'. The difference between data and information is a pretty crucial one for the manager. It points up the fallacy in the old saying 'the facts speak for themselves'. The facts speak only to those who understand their language. If the manager hasn't the background knowledge to make out what they're telling him, all he has got is a load of data, not information. He 'knows' the facts but can't use them to take intelligent decisions.

Many managers criticise this kind of knowledge as useless — whether it's the simple knowledge of a subject without the practical ability to apply it, or the simple knowledge of data that can't be properly interpreted for lack of understanding of the subject. They think it's better not to burden themselves with such knowledge. But they misunderstand the problem. The answer is to learn more about the subject, not to discard the knowledge they have. And most of that extra knowledge comes from actually getting involved in trying to use whatever knowledge you've already got. It's the knowhow you get from experience.

Level 4: Knowhow

You know the knowledge and can apply it. You are familiar enough with the way the labour costing method actually does operate to understand the problem and to work out a practical way of tackling it. You can also see when and how the accountants will need to be involved. You understand the purpose of the system well enough to help find a solution that both they and you can accept.

This is the level of knowledge you need before you can use your commonsense. Commonsense is sometimes thought of as something you can apply to subjects that you don't know much about, as when a manager tries to explain something to one of his staff and then says 'if you're not sure about it, use your commonsense'. But in fact you need a good practical knowledge of a subject before you can bring commonsense to bear. You need to know what's important and what isn't so that you don't get sidetracked by unimportant details. You also have to know what's possible and what isn't, what causes what effects, what kinds of things can create problems. Commonsense is essential in most management thinking and decision-making, but it can't teach you things you don't know about a subject.

Level 5: Full understanding
You can both apply the knowledge and develop it further. You understand the principles of labour costing so well that you can think constructively about the present method. You can see why it is designed in the way it is, and can question that purpose intelligently to find a better principle of design. You can create ideas about modifications to it that not only overcome your problem but even make the method a better one from an accountancy viewpoint. At this level of knowledge you can discuss the question with the accountants on equal terms to find an answer that is both sound financial practice and effective for your operation.

If a manager sees his job as improving the way his area operates, he needs this level of knowledge about the things he is directly responsible for. At the knowhow level he knows what has worked in the past. To reach a fuller understanding of what is possible in the future, he has to look afresh at familiar situations and question existing methods: 'why do we do this?' 'why deal with it this way?' 'what is the real purpose?' 'how could we do it differently?' 'what would be the consequences?' Such thinking demands a grasp of principles, an understanding of how theory relates to practice. It's a common view of practical managers that all theorising is rubbish because it won't work in the real world. But that's a theory in itself, and not a very good one. A poor theory is unworkable, but there's nothing as practical as a good theory. Ask Barnes Wallis!

The ladder of knowledge is a progression. When you first become aware of something, you realise that knowledge of its existence had been available all along. It didn't suddenly spring into being when you discovered it. And you might also realise that other people's states of knowledge about it are ranged all the way up the ladder. Some are in your previous state of total ignorance. Others are ahead of you — some with simple knowledge that they can't really apply, some with practical knowhow, and perhaps just a few with a full understanding of the subject and the capacity to create further knowledge about it.

How do you climb this ladder? Primarily by developing the habit of asking yourself questions that prompt you to search for the knowledge. Ask the *right* questions and they become important direction-finders to the sort of knowledge that's relevant. Rudyard Kipling summed up the idea in a few lines of verse:

'I have six honest serving men,
They taught me all I knew.
Their names are WHAT? and HOW? and WHEN?
And WHY? and WHERE? and WHO?'

That's not all there is to it of course. Kipling's questions have to be filled out a bit, depending on the subject:

WHAT is happening here? What is actually going on? What is important about it? What else does it link with? In what way does it concern me?

HOW does it happen? How does it work? How do the principles behind it operate? How much do I need to know about it?

WHEN does it happen? When did it start? When does it become important? When are its consequences likely to become apparent? When do I need to know?

WHY does it happen? Why is it needed? Why does it work in this way or that? Why should I find out more — to what use can I put my knowledge?

WHERE does it happen — in what circumstances? Where do its effects appear? Where can I get more information about it?

WHO is involved — and what are their concerns? Who else is affected? Who can best tell me what I need to know?

Managers sometimes complain of not having enough information for their decision-making. Perhaps it's more often a problem of not having the right information. Especially in large organisations, the fact of the matter is usually that they have too much information. They're inundated with it. The real shortage is a lack of the questions that the information is needed to answer. And it's up to the managers themselves to define the questions that need answering.

Some years ago there was a BBC television series called *The Troubleshooters* — episodes in the life of a fictional oil company called Mogul Oil. One episode was about a disaster to one of the company's overseas installations, an explosion and fire that had wrecked half a refinery. An executive flew out from London headquarters for a preliminary investigation. There followed a long-distance telephone call in which he reported back to his Managing Director. The Managing Director asked a total of five questions, each one short and to the point. The executive answered them one by one, and in a mere minute and a half of screen time the whole situation was clear. Fiction of course, but in real life whose skill was the crucial one illustrated?

Just one further point on question-asking. You usually have to know a certain amount about a subject before your questions on it become very sensible. This is quite an important point when managers consult someone who has expert knowledge in a field that concerns them — say an accountant, or a personnel or training specialist, or a consultant perhaps. They are terribly prone to rely on the expert's ability to solve their problem without their having to learn anything about his subject. What they forget is that if the expert knows next to nothing about *their* operation, his expertise may create as many problems for them as it solves. *Someone* has to get far enough into the other's field to know what are sensible questions to ask about it. And nearly always it's easier for the managers to get an adequate idea of the expert's subject than the other way round. In any case the expert will usually be less motivated to try to understand all the ramifications of what goes on in their departments. There's also the principle of managerial responsibility at stake. The managers must be able to question intelligently what the expert proposes and satisfy themselves about it, otherwise their responsiblity is a sham.

B. The skills of thinking

The first thing to accept is that instant thinking is rather like instant soup. There's usually little meat in it. Thinking needs time — real thinking that is, rather than grabbing at bright ideas or 'obvious' answers. Far too many managers rush into decisions without giving themselves time to think out the problems they are trying to solve. Their real thinking follows their decisions when they try to rationalise them. They will plunge into a disciplinary interview with a fixed idea of the misdemeanour they are tackling and spend most of the interview justifying the solution they've already decided on. Faced with an emergency, they will take a snap decision that causes them problem after problem as its consequences become clear.

Good thinking doesn't jump to conclusions. It identifies the questions that should be asked, searches around for possibilities, considers the implications of ideas — and suspends judgement meanwhile. That disciplinary interview: was it really dealing with a piece of negligence? Perhaps a little bit of investigation might show that the subordinate needs some guidance rather than disciplining. Or perhaps the situation he was in at the time explains his behaviour. Even if he was deliberately flouting a rule, is the objective to punish or to ensure the rule is willingly followed in the future? That emergency: would a few moments thought have been impossible? Perhaps the decision wasn't that urgent. Or perhaps the immediate decision should have been a temporising answer rather than a firm and final solution.

But even given time, managers can still show a lack of skill in the thinking they apply to the problems, questions and decisions they have to deal with. There are two common limitations in their thinking technique. The first is a natural human tendency to see a situation from only one point of view rather than trying to look at it from a variety of angles. This often makes it impossible to understand the situation fully, in the same way as a photograph of a statue fails to reveal its full shape. The second limitation is to take too restricted a field of view. This means that things that are relevant to a situation are left outside the thinking that's done about it, like the photograph of a holiday hotel that fails to show the industrial estate next door.

Most skills involve getting conscious control of things that are uncontrolled in the unskilled person's performance. It's the same for skill in thinking. It comes from deliberately trying to adopt different angles of view on a subject, and becoming conscious of the fences that restrict the field of thinking about it. One can then consciously enlarge the field.

Finding different angles

As you think about a situation you inevitably slip into a certian way of looking at it. This is not because you choose to do so. It is because of the way the brain works — you cannot help doing it. The particular angle you take up depends on many things. What you first noticed about the situation, your past experiences, your expectations, your interests and concerns, your attitudes, the way the subject fits in with other knowledge you have — all of these play their part. Nearly always this is an unconscious mental process.

The result is to create for you a personal 'centre of attention' in the situation. One aspect of it, one part of the total situation becomes the area that unconsciously you focus on and that creates the 'meaning' of the situation for you. This may sound terribly complicated and difficult, so let's try to illustrate the point.

What do you see? The head of a young woman half turned away from you? Or the face of an old crone half turned towards you? Many people when they first look at the picture can see only one woman, and find it quite impossible to make their minds switch to the other — even if they know she's there. The longer they go on looking the harder it becomes to break away from the first 'meaning' they saw. Which is exactly what might be expected to happen. Once you have understood a subject in one way, you start to become conditioned to see it in the same way whenever the subject reappears. You develop what the psychologists call a 'mental set'.

The thing that creates and confirms this mental set is whatever you focus on as the centre of your attention. In this case, it's the bit of the picture your eye happens to centre on that decides which of the two women you see:

> The young woman? Your eye has centred on the tip of her nose and her eyelashes beyond the line of her cheek. Your peripheral vision converts the rest into supporting evidence for the picture you've seen — her earring, the line of her jaw, her neckband.

> The old crone? Your eye has centred on her baggy eye. Peripheral vision now interprets the rest in a different way — her nose and nostril, the bag under her hidden eye, thin mouth, protruding chin.

Once you know the trick you can force your mind into either interpretation at will — simply by fixing your gaze on the appropriate point.

In fact there's rather more than this to the way the mind interprets a subject. Often the interpretation doesn't depend on what you focus on but on the angle of view that your mind assumes:

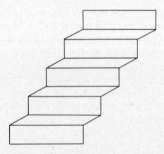

A staircase. But from which angle are you looking at it? From above or below? Again there are two interpretations, but now it's not a question of what you focus on but the position in which you assume you're standing.

In thinking about anything, your mind is always

unconsciously doing this centering and adopting an angle of view. And this restricts the scope of your thinking about it. It's like seeing only one of the women, only one point of view on the staircase — and then assuming that that is all there is in each picture.

One of the skills of thinking is to deliberately switch your focus on whatever you are thinking about, to force yourself to see it from angles that you wouldn't otherwise adopt. This isn't a thing our brains do naturally, no more than our bodies naturally perform the movement of a gymnast. In a manager's thinking, the natural process tends to do this sort of thing:

- He hits a difficulty in trying to solve a problem. The difficulty is inevitable with the solution he has picked on, and there's no good answer to it. But because his mind is now focussed on that particular solution, he persists in trying to think of ways around the difficulty. A different view of the original problem would show there is another, far easier solution, but his thinking is now too fixated for him to see the problem that way.

- A subordinate suggests an idea. Perhaps because of the way the idea is presented, the manager sees a flaw in it. This creates his focus in the idea as a whole and his view of it shapes up in a negative way. Any good points in the idea either disappear or are devalued in his thinking. He is now incapable of thinking constructively about it.

The thinking skills that avoid mental limitations like these can be practiced initially as drills. For example, in thinking about the subordinate's idea, there is Edward de Bono's tool the drill of 'Plus, Minus and Interesting'. Before making any judgement on whether the idea is good or bad, you spend a few minutes looking for all its plus-points — its advantages, benefits, gains. Then you switch your focus to spend a few minutes looking for minus-points — its disadvantages, snags, difficulties. Finally, you do a mental search for any other features of the idea which are neither plus nor minus points — interesting questions it raises, possible ways of developing it and so on. Once you've done this, you are far better placed to make a rational, objective judgement about the value of the idea.

Managers may argue they do this sort of thing anyway. So

*These tools come from the CoRT Thinking Lessons published by Pergamon Press, Oxford and also from the book 'de Bono's Course in Thinking.' (BBC Publications).

they do — sometimes, but even then not in a disciplined kind of way. The point of the mental drill is to build a habit of adopting first one focus, then another, *before* making your mind up.

Enlarging the field of view

You are planning to change a system of operation in your section. You've thought about the plusses and minuses of the idea, and can be certain that the change will make your staff's work more efficient. So you get down to the details and discuss with your people how the new arrangement will be implemented. A chance conversation with a manager in another department makes you suddenly aware that the change will cause difficulties there — difficulties you might have realised if you'd thought of the implications outside your own section. It just hadn't occurred to you to think of them. Now you're in a fix. You've committed yourself to the change and your staff's morale will suffer if you go back on the idea. If you go ahead, you'll lose the cooperation you need from that other department.

In one form or another, this kind of mental block is quite common. As a manager recognises a problem, he unconsciously draws a fence around it that confines his thinking. Many of the problems he deals with are tackled quite successfully within the mental fences he constructs. So he tends not to look at the fence itself as a difficulty when he has a problem that can't be solved inside it.

Here's a simple illustration of this snag in the thinking process. It's a problem called 'The Nine-dot Square':

$$
\begin{matrix}
\bullet & \bullet & \bullet \\
\bullet & \bullet & \bullet \\
\bullet & \bullet & \bullet
\end{matrix}
$$

The problem is to draw four straight lines to connect all nine dots in the square *without removing the pen from the paper*. The lines may cross. If your pen retraces a line you've already drawn, that counts as a further line.

People usually begin by drawing around the sides of the square — and then realise this leaves the central dot unconnected. So then try drawing lines inside the square, diagonals and so on. Their successive attempts often look like these:

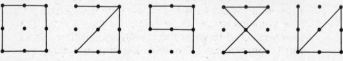

144

. . . at which point some start to say 'it can't be done'. It can. But to do it you have first to 'get over the fence' that the *idea* of a square creates in the mind. The answer is very simple, even obvious, once you've enlarged the field of your thinking to include the space *outside* the square:

The kind of thinking that's involved is a question of becoming conscious of a fence you've put up in your mind, and then deliberately going outside it to explore a wider range of possibilities.

In management the fences are many. They are erected by words like 'finance', 'industrial relations', 'training', 'organisation and methods'. The manager who uses one of them to label a problem he's got is quite likely to start regarding it as 'outside my field' rather than thinking it through for himself. The structure of an organisation creates further mental fences — 'production' and 'purchasing' and 'sales' and 'distribution'. But a problem that pops up in one of these fields may well have its roots in another. It may even lie at the point where they meet. Which is why it pays the manager to increase his knowledge of aspects of his organisation that may at first sight seem not to concern him directly. His understanding of a problem that *does* concern him may depend on his ability to 'think over the fences' into other areas.

When managers unconsciously let their thinking become too narrow, it's not unusual to find them tackling the wrong problem:

– in a research department, section leaders had to write monthly progress reports on their sections' work. The reports were criticised by their managers as poorly written — their contents were scrappy and seemed to be badly thought out. The problem was defined as 'poor communication skills' and report-writing courses were arranged. These revealed a different problem. The section leaders did not know how their reports were used and so had no basis on which to judge what information was needed. Also no time was allocated in their work-programmes for preparing the reports. They were expected to write them in their own time. The word 'communication' had blinkered their managers' view of the problem and stopped them from searching for the real reason for the poor reports they were getting.

- the drive shaft of a machine in an engineering works was repeatedly fracturing. Each time its makers were called in to replace the shaft. Each time their machine came under hotter criticism from the works management for faulty design. They spent a lot of time and effort trying to track down the design fault and even redesigned the shaft for one of the replacements. This fractured too. The cost was mounting — both the cost to themselves of free-of-charge work and the cost to their customer of having the machine out of service. Quite by accident, a service engineer working on the fifth replacement noticed something odd about the plinth on which the machine was mounted. This foundation (which was the customer's responsibility) had been prepared by subcontractors. It turned out to be an old one with a thin surface of fresh concrete skimmed over it. As a result the machine had not been properly bedded down, and when running it vibrated heavily enough to fracture the shaft. The idea 'design fault' had been enough to stop anyone involved looking further afield for the real cause of the problem.

You may think the managers concerned in both these incidents were a bit stupid, but that's because you now know the answers. They were intelligent people. But they had followed that natural human inclination to assume that a problem is understood without thinking much about it. We tend to be more interested in the thinking that goes into finding solutions than the thinking that's needed for understanding problems. But often it's an over-narrow idea of a problem that creates difficulties in finding a good solution.

There are mental drills for developing the skill of enlarging the field of thinking about a subject. One of the most simple and effective is another of Edward de Bono's tools* the drill of 'Consider All Factors'. It means taking a few minutes to think about anything that could conceivably have a bearing on the problem or question you're dealing with. And you do this without making any judgements about the things that occur to you — they all go into the pot to be sorted out later. You're searching for ideas, not trying to decide their importance or

*These tools come from the CoRT Thinking Lessons published by Pergamon Press, Oxford and also from the book 'de Bono's Course in Thinking.' (BBC Publications).

value. The one question you're focussing on in those few minutes is 'What else haven't I thought of?'

This may sound obvious, but *we don't do it naturally*. It's a human tendency to want certainty and decisiveness in our thinking, particularly when we're in a hurry to get to the action — which managers often are. Mental fences make us more secure in dealing with the subjects inside them. They allow us to feel we know what is 'relevant', and simply not to think of anything outside. Automatically it becomes irrelevant in our thinking.

The difficulty in enlarging the field of view isn't one of exploring for ideas. Once we've got started, the ideas are usually there. The real difficulty is that it doesn't occur to us to set out and look for them — and that's why the drill is necessary to help develop the mental habit.

Combining the skills

If you learn a skill like driving a car or playing the piano, you have to begin by dividing it up into separate bits of skill. At first you need to practice each one independently — you can't cope with them all together. In the car you learn where to find the controls. You get the hang of using clutch and accelerator to start it moving. You try to cope with changing gear. But meanwhile your steering is likely to be fairly erratic, so your instructor doesn't let you get into tricky situations that require skill in that department. Similarly for the piano: simple scales for each hand in turn, then we'll try both hands together . . .

It's the same for developing skills in thinking. There are drills that enable you to practice the different skills one at a time. But a lot of real thinking has to combine them. Edward de Bono's story* illustrates how the skills of finding different angles and enlarging the field of view might sometimes have to be combined.

A merchant in ancient times owed a large sum to a moneylender which he could not repay. According to the law of the land, the moneylender had the right to have the merchant thrown into jail for debt, but he thought to turn the situation to some personal advantage. He had heard that the merchant had a beautiful daughter. He himself had long wanted to marry, but was exceedingly ugly and no woman would accept him.

He arranged to meet the merchant and his daughter in a garden nearby to make his proposal: if the girl would marry him, the merchant would have his freedom. His proposal was

* From Edward de Bono's book 'The Use of Lateral Thinking' (Penguin Books)

rejected, but he had conceived another idea. He would propose a game of chance for the girl's hand in marriage. If she agreed to it, he would free the merchant from his debt however the game turned out. The three of them were standing in the middle of a broad path that ran through the garden. Its surface was covered with a loose mixture of pebbles, some black and some white. For the game he proposed, he would pick up two pebbles, one white and one black, and put them in an empty leather moneybag he had with him. The girl would then put her hand into the bag and take out one pebble. If it was the black pebble she would marry him if the white one she would be free.

The girl eventually decided to accept the chance. The moneylender bent down, picked up two pebbles and swiftly placed them in the bag — but not before the girl's sharp eyes had seen what he had done. He had put two *black* pebbles into the bag.

Whichever pebble she takes out her fate is sealed. Or is it?

The way people try to think out this problem produces all sorts of unsatisfactory ideas. She picks up a white pebble and conceals it in her hand — can you see the moneylender falling for that one? She pulls out both pebbles to show he has cheated — whereupon he says 'it was only a game, but your father goes to jail'. Some ideas are adequate but not very pleasant for the girl. She marries the moneylender for the sake of his money — but she isn't mercenary and she loathes him. She marries him for the sake of her father — full marks to her for loyalty, but would her father agree?

There's a very simple solution. But the ability to think of it depends on the girl doing two things simultaneously in her mind: changing the centre of her attention in the problem, and enlarging her field of view to take in a factor that is at first sight 'outside the problem'.

Consider the problem she starts with: it is contained in the bag, and eventually it will centre on the pebble she'll be holding. That's what she 'sees' in her mind, and it's unlikely with the emotional pressure she's under that she'll be able to start thinking further. The solution for her may begin with a pure accident — she fumbles and drops the pebble as she takes it out.

Now rethink the problem: the outside factor is the path she's standing on. Once the pebble has fallen it is lost among the other pebbles there. All she has to do now is to change the focus of her attention: 'but you can tell which one I had — you've still got the other one left in the bag'.

Management situations sometimes give opportunities for a combination of thinking skills like this. The ideas that emerge may look very simple, even obvious. But nothing is really obvious until someone has thought of it. The real skill of the thinker can often be really appreciated only by others who have tried to think through the same problem, with the same knowledge as is available to him, and who have failed to find a solution that's as good as his. Even then their own ego-defences may lead them to accuse him of 'cheating' or to look only for the snags to his solution.

Improving your thinking

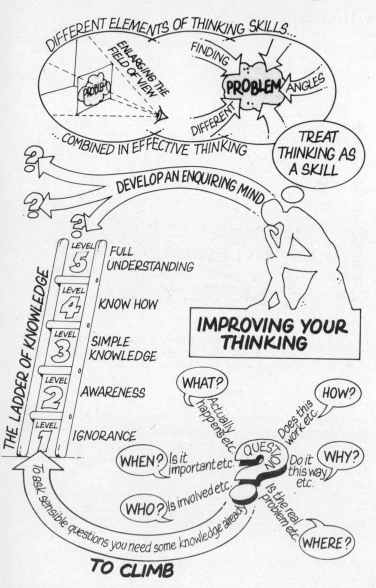

13. Edward de Bono's thinking tools*

Edward de Bono is becoming widely known for his books, television series and teaching programmes on the skills of thinking. Single-handed he has developed a great deal of the practical knowledge that is available on how thinking can be learned. But his name may not be as familiar to you as the general term he coined for the kinds of thinking skill we've been considering — 'Lateral Thinking'. It sums up the mental processes that are needed to explore a subject.

De Bono has developed a number of drills, or 'tools' as he calls them, that can be practised to improve those thinking skills. Two of them have been mentioned — 'Plus, Minus and Interesting' and 'Consider All Factors'. There are many others, and a lot of them combine the different skills in various ways. The purpose of each one is to nudge one's thinking in a different direction from the one which the tramlines in the mind are likely to take it:

*These tools come from the CoRT Thinking Lessons published by Pergamon Press, Oxford and also from the book 'de Bono's Course in Thinking.' (BBC Publications).

'Alternatives, Possibilities, Choices': one of the most important tools to prompt the search for ideas. All it involves is taking the time to think of alternatives in a situation you're dealing with. There's no special significance in the three words. They all stand for the same kind of thinking, but in different circumstances one or another of them might be the most appropriate.

The exercise might be done when there's a decision to take — what choices do you have between different courses of action? It might help generate ideas about causes of a problem or about ways of solving it — what alternatives should you consider? Often it can stimulate thinking about a situation or activity that doesn't seem to contain any problem — what other possibilities are there for handling it? Its purpose is to combat the universal tendency not to *start* thinking about such things if an apparently adequate idea already exists. Satisfaction with the merely adequate is both poor thinking and poor management.

'Consequence and Sequel': a tool to counter the natural inclination to very short-term thinking. It involves thinking out the possible effects of an action or decision (or a *non*-action for that matter) in three stages: in the short-term, middle-term and long-term future. To use it, the first thing is to decide how to define these periods — is 'short-term' for instance to be during the next few days, the next month or so, or within a year? Obviously, this will depend on the kind of question you are dealing with. Once you've decided the time-periods, you focus on each period in turn and speculate what consequences might appear within that time.

Of course there is nothing certain about the ideas you get. The value of the exercise lies in deliberately trying to think ahead in a specific and disciplined way about something that concerns you as a manager.

'Information-In and Information-Out': a tool to overcome the frequent failure to consider what one *doesn't* know about a situation one is dealing with. To use it you first assess the information you *have* got. You look at its relevance and see what it actually tells you about the situation. You then see what it *cannot* tell you, trying to avoid the common tendency to make assumptions about things we don't in fact know. You define the questions that are relevant but that can't be answered with the information you have.

It may well be that once you've defined the questions, you realise it *is* possible to get answers to some of them. But nearly always there will be questions that you cannot get answers to.

152

The point of the exercise is to make yourself as conscious as you can of those gaps in your knowledge so that you can make allowances for them in your thinking.

'Examine Both Sides': a tool to use before getting involved in negotiations or in dealing with a conflict of views. When faced with a view opposed to one's own, nearly everyone is reluctant to explore it. Sometimes this may be because of a conviction that the view is totally wrong and there is nothing in it worth exploring. Sometimes it may be caused by a fear that it might reduce one's commitment to one's own view. The purpose of the exercise is to conquer this reluctance. In doing it, you look first at your own and then at your opponent's viewpoints. In each case you think through the reasons *why* each of you holds his particular view — trying to be equally objective about your reasons and his. The essential idea is to be neutral in doing this examination so that you can get a clear view of the real issues involved.

'Agreement, Disagreement and Irrelevance': the use of this tool follows directly on from an 'Examine Both Sides' exercise. It involves first listing all the issues that both sides can agree on, then the issues that they disagree about, and finally other points that might well be raised but are in fact irrelevant to the argument.

Often it is worthwhile to see a disagreement in the context of what are nearly always far larger areas of agreement. During an argument these areas seem to be smaller than they actually are, simply because one's thinking is focussed on the disagreements. Irrelevancies are often used for point-scoring. The effect of mapping out the areas beforehand is to enable you to get such things into perspective. It helps you to think more coolly and rationally as the argument develops.

'Other People's Views': this tool has a more general use than the previous one. As a manager, you will often find yourself dealing with a situation in which a number of different people have differing interests. Their interests may not conflict, but a decision that suits some may not suit others. The problem is that you may overlook some of these different interests when you take your decisions.

The exercise is done before you reach the decision-point. Its first step is to identify the other people concerned. Then, taking the point of view of each person or group in turn, you look at the situation as they are likely to see it and note what their interests are likely to be. This gives you a list of criteria for your decision to try and satisfy — and makes it more likely that the decision will be a fair one from everyone's point of view.

'High Value — Low Value': this tool has a more subtle purpose than the others we've listed, and is often more difficult to use. But it deals with a very important element in many management decisions. Everyone's attitudes and decisions are influenced by their personal values. They give us a basis for our judgements of other people's behaviour. They govern what we see as important in a situation. They make us willing to act in one way, loth to act in another. They sometimes conflict with each other — for instance when we find a decision a difficult one to make. But usually in thinking about a situation, we don't consciously consider our values. Even though they have a fundamental effect on the way we think about it, they are left in the background.

In a 'High Value — Low Value' exercise, you look *directly* at the personal values that are involved in a situation you have to deal with. You say what they are (which is often quite a difficult exercise in itself). Having done so, you consider how far each one of them will influence the way you handle the situation. You divide them into:

> — High Value: the values that will decide what you do.
> — Low Value: the values that you'll take into account but won't be decisive.

The exercise demands you to be ruthlessly honest with yourself. It may also give you some problems in deciding whether a factor is really a high-value one for you or a low-value one. But this is really the point of the exercise. It gets you to *examine your values*.

One of the advantages of the total is that it combats the emotional effects of value-laden *words* that are so often brought into play during arguments. Often the same situation can look very different when it is presented in different words: 'I am firm, you are obstinate, he is a pig-headed fool'. The feelings caused by positive and negative-flavoured words frequently prevent clear thinking. But if you have objectively considered the values really involved, it is easier to avoid having your thinking distorted by such emotional pressures.

You might well consider all these tools very simple and obvious. So they are. But that doesn't mean they are not useful. Each one acts as an instruction to yourself to start thinking about a situation in a particular way — a way that is quite likely not to occur to you otherwise. It gets you to think, not just about the situation, but also about *the kind of thinking* you are applying to it. And if you make yourself familiar with the range of tools available to you, they act as reminders of the different kinds of thinking that might be useful in one situation or another. You can then say to yourself 'at this point I should do a 'Consider All Factors' exercise', or 'now I should think of 'Alternatives, Possibilities, Choices'''.

Thinking about one's thinking in this way is not something we do naturally, no more than we think about the way we breathe or walk. But if you regard thinking as a skill you become conscious of the way you're doing it, in the same way as a singer thinks about his breathing or a long-distance walker makes himself aware of how he walks. As a manager, your thinking is an important part of your repertoire of management abilities. To think about the way you're doing it is a necessary first step to improving your skill. That's the value of these tools to you.

Tools for thinking

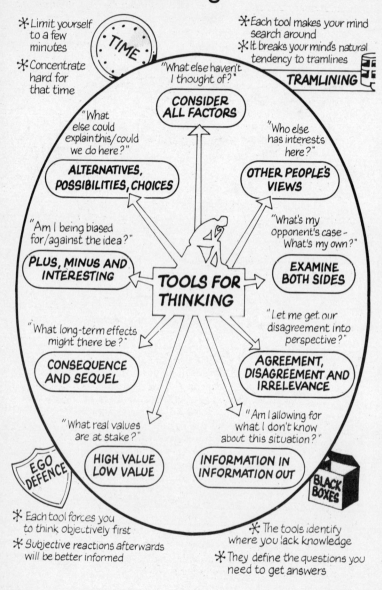

* Limit yourself to a few minutes
* Concentrate hard for that time

TIME

* Each tool makes your mind search around
* It breaks your mind's natural tendency to tramlines

TRAMLINING

"What else haven't I thought of?"

CONSIDER ALL FACTORS

"What else could explain this/could we do here?"

ALTERNATIVES, POSSIBILITIES, CHOICES

"Who else has interests here?"

OTHER PEOPLE'S VIEWS

"Am I being biased for/against the idea?"

PLUS, MINUS AND INTERESTING

"What's my opponent's case - What's my own?"

EXAMINE BOTH SIDES

TOOLS FOR THINKING

"Let me get our disagreement into perspective?"

"What long-term effects might there be?"

CONSEQUENCE AND SEQUEL

AGREEMENT, DISAGREEMENT AND IRRELEVANCE

"Am I allowing for what I don't know about this situation?"

"What real values are at stake?"

HIGH VALUE LOW VALUE

INFORMATION IN INFORMATION OUT

BLACK BOXES

EGO DEFENCE

* Each tool forces you to think objectively first
* Subjective reactions afterwards will be better informed

* The tools identify where you lack knowledge
* They define the questions you need to get answers

14. Organising the thinking

Lateral thinking is de Bono's general term for the 'search-type' thinking we've been discussing. It's important, and often it's exactly the kind of thinking that gets blocked-off by ego-defences and tramlining. But it's not the only kind there is.

The other sort of thinking is 'logic-type' thinking that's usually needed to make the results of mental searches usable. Take the job of preparing a report for example. It begins with a search for the information and ideas you can consider as possible subject matter. Alongside this are other kinds of search to do — to identify the readers, to decide what the report's aim and emphasis should be, to think of the questions you should be trying to answer. But once you've done all this, the report has still to be written. You now have to switch to a different kind of thinking: how will you arrange the content? What should you start the report with? In what order will you put the information? How will you lay it all out? Logical thinking has to be done at some stage in most managerial work.

Logical thinking too has skills. There are two basic ones that apply to most forms of thinking when you are trying to sort out the things you've already sought of:
- sectioning
- sequencing.

A. Sectioning

A mass of facts or ideas becomes a mess. So that the mind can make sense of it, it has to find a way of dividing it up. To understand or control something that's all complicated involves separating its elements into related sections:
- a series of paragraphs in a letter.
- a scheme of headings in a report.
- a plan of discussion-points in a meeting.
- an office filing system.
- a supermarket's arrangement of goods on the shelves.
- the abilities into which management can be divided for study — planning, organising, controlling, etc.
- the structure of jobs and departments in an organisation.
- any system of knowledge like engineering, mathematics, psychology, economics, accountancy etc.
- the aspects of a problem.
- the English language itself, which is really a system (though a hugely complex one) of analysing the things we observe and the store of memory.

Sectioning is the process by which the brain organises its fields of knowledge or thinking. To make sense of any random collection of facts and ideas, you have to try to understand their inter-relationships. You see where one item matches with another and where items don't match, so that you know what to put with what else and where to draw the dividing lines. If you *can't* find a pattern of sections, you can't see any 'sense' in the subject. The more clear-cut and coherent the pattern is, the more manageable do the facts and ideas become.

For a lot of the time, we can use ready-made sectioning systems — standard formulas that other people have already worked out. This is much easier than working them out for ourselves. But we cannot always avoid the need to develop our own methods of organising things. In many a letter or report, the subject-matter won't fall neatly into a pre-arranged format. In many a plan, the actions can't be arranged in a text-book pattern. In many an organisation structure the responsibilities can't be allocated to people along orthodox principles. In situations like this, the skill of logical sectioning is as important as the skills of search-type thinking.

In fact both kinds of skill have to be used. One starts with the imaginative thinking that's needed to see different possibilities for sectioning. But then you have to check out each possibility with the question 'would this work logically?' A logical system of sections has five main features:

1. Each section is clearly distinct from all the other sections. The system follows the principle of mutual exclusion — whatever goes into one section *couldn't* be logically put into any of the others. The topics of the different sections interlink but they don't overlap. Each section can be given a label (a title or heading) that applies only to its own subject-matter.

2. All the sections taken together cover the whole subject. The system doesn't leave any stray bits of the subject out of account, to be collected perhaps in a kind of 'dustbin' section. In report-writing, it avoids the mess that's indicated by a heading like 'Miscellaneous' or 'Some Further Thoughts'. In an organisation structure, it doesn't create the need for ' General Handyman' jobs that contain a lot of bitty tasks and activities. In a meeting it doesn't leave important issues to be hastily scrambled through in an 'Any Other Business' item at the end of the agenda. Everything has a proper home.

3. The different sections are all related together in a consistent way. The system uses one, and only one, principle of division to separate its sections one from another. For instance, the jobs of a number of salesmen might be divided by the geographical areas they cover *or* the types of customers they call on *or* the products they sell. But in a logical system, you can't have some jobs defined by the areas covered, some by the customers visited and some by the products sold. If you do have a mess like this, be prepared for all sorts of problems of coordination.

4. The system contains a limited number of sections, usually not more than five or six. With more than seven, it becomes almost impossible for the brain to understand how they hang together. In fact the main point of sectioning is to limit the number of things you have to relate together in your mind. If in reading a long report you had mentally to link every statement to every other statement before you could understand the report, you'd have an impossible task. The report's system of headings allows you instead to relate 'lumps' of statements to each other,

159

which is easier. Even so, if there are too many 'lumps', you'll still find the report confusing.

The real problem is the huge number of relationships that can exist between even a few inter-related things. To see the size of the problem think for example of the relationships between different numbers of people who are working together:

- two people, two relationships — how A sees B, how B sees A.
- three people, twelve relationships. Now there are not only the individual relationships between A and B, B and C, C and A. There is also the way C affects the relationship between A and B and the way he is affected *by* it (the 'Gooseberry Effect') etc.
- four people, forty-eight relationships between individuals, pairs, threesomes. Arithmetic has to help now: multiply the last number of relationships you had (twelve) by the number of people you've now got (four). And so on for increasing numbers:
- five people, 240 relationships
- six people, 1440 relationships
- seven people, 10,080 relationships.

It's not that you have to be conscious of all these relationships to understand them — the brain probably does a lot of this subconsciously. But there is a limit. With a number of items that goes beyond that limit, you become aware of a problem in 'holding it all together' in your mind.

5. The system of sectioning is one that suits a particular purpose. This is a rather different kind of point from the others. They were saying that the system must be able to cope with the subject-matter in a logical way. This one looks at what you're using the subject-matter *for.* It says that your system must emphasise those aspects of the total subject that are most important for whatever you are trying to do. For example, in a report the scheme of headings should allow the *key* points of information to be stressed. In a meeting, the way the chairman divides up a subject into different areas of discussion should enable everyone present to concentrate on the *key* issues they have to resolve. In an organisation the structure of departments, sections and teams should make it easy for people to coordinate their efforts to achieve the *key* aims of the organisation as a whole. However neat and logical a system may look, it's a poor one if it doesn't organise its subject-matter effectively for *use.*

There is one further essential point to remember about any system of mentally dividing up a collection of things — whether they are objects or information or activities of people. The system itself is only a convenient way of understanding or controlling them. The sections aren't 'real'. Nor are the divisions between them. Don't fall into the trap of thinking that the things you've grouped together are actually the same — and that they're *actually* different from the things in other sections.

For instance, if you divide the people in an organisation into 'managers' and 'workers', don't start thinking they are really different sorts of human beings. They are different only in certain things they do, that's all. Once he has made the distinction, many a manager seems to suppose they really are different animals: 'managers' are all dedicated to their work (or ought to be), 'workers' all have to be pushed; 'managers' can understand things but 'workers' can't; 'managers' have good judgement but 'workers' haven't, and so on. This sort of thinking is a gross mis-use of the mental skill of logical sectioning.

This book has made quite an issue of ways of sectioning various things to emphasise their differences. There were the differences between managers and businessmen, administrators, accountants and the others — differences in their approaches to the workings of an organisation, in what they see as important, in the kinds of questions they ask. But don't let that fool you into thinking that a collection of people can be neatly categorised into those various disciplines. Some administrators are pretty effective managers. Many an accountant has a lot of the qualities that go to make a successful businessman. It would be a mistake to suppose that their brains are somehow constructed differently or that they are incapable of thinking intelligently about each others' disciplines. Put a number of them together, and there are lots of possible ways you could divide them that have nothing to do with the distinctions between their professional abilities.

The same goes for the differences between the management priorities — work, money and people. The point of that analysis was to overcome the common tendency to overlook one or another of them. But all three have to be welded together in the way a manager thinks about his responsibilities. He can't treat them as though they were independent of each other. Similarly for the skills of planning, organising, motivating and so on. They are deployed together in most managerial decision-making. The only purpose in separating them is to make it easier to identify a skill that needs some development.

Skill in sectioning is an essential part of the most logical thinking — the skill of spotting similarities and differences. But part of the skill is in recognising how far any particular system of sectioning things is valid and useful. If you start to suppose that the divisions somehow represent differences between the essential natures of the things themselves, you're stuck in mental tramlines that will make your thinking unrealistic.

B. Sequencing

A great deal of thinking involves making a string of logical connections: 'because this, therefore that, and so the other, but that means so-and-so, which can't be done because I have such-and-such to consider . . .' In fact this 'follow-on' sort of thinking is the most common kind of thought-pattern we use. Embedded in our language are lots of little words whose only purpose is to make these connections: 'and', 'so', 'but', 'because' 'for instance', 'unless', 'if', 'then' and all the rest.

It's natural to think in sequences. From one event to another in a 'what-happens-next' time-sequence. From a situation we've become aware of, to a problem in it and on to a solution. From something we want to do to the actions that might achieve it. From an incident to a general principle that lies behind it — or the other way round, from a principle to particular examples of how it operates. From something that has happened back to what might have caused it — or again, the other way about, from something that might happen forward to its consequences and then the consequences of those consequences.

Skill in sequencing is particularly important in the shared thinking that we call 'communicating'. But even though thinking in sequences is very familiar to all of us, quite a lot of people — managers included — don't seem to be very skilful at thinking about *how* they are sequencing things in their minds. A meeting for instance may have several inter-connected questions to deal with which it is necessary to take in a certain order. Most of us have experienced the problems caused by a chairman who gets it wrong — who tries to discuss solutions before problems have been thrashed out, who wastes time on minor points and then has to rush the discussion of major ones, who fails to see how one issue is relevant to another. Or there's the manager who muddles through an explanation of something because he hasn't got his thoughts properly ordered. He plunges into the middle of his subject, then realises something else has to be explained first — and while doing so sees that even that can't be understood without an explanation of yet another thing . . . As points occur to him he hops backwards and forwards and sideways around his subject, confusing both his audience and himself. This clearly won't do. When the time comes to involve others in your thinking, it's usually essential to find a good, logical order to follow.

The most important thing for logical sequencing is to find the right starting point. If you don't do that, it's often impossible to get into a train of thought that reaches the right conclusions. *Before* you begin to think about a solution to a problem, are you sure you've got a correct understanding of the problem itself? *Before* you try to pin down the problem, have you really thought hard enough about the situation in which the problem lies? Do you need to go even further back in finding your starting point — to the events that led up to the situation or to your broad aims in handling it? Often there's nothing wrong with the actual step-by-step development of a manager's sequence of thoughts about a subject. The thing that's wrong is his starting point. He's like the traveller in the Irish story who gets a response to his request for directions to his destination: 'if I were you, sor, I wouldn't start from here'.

Sequencing and sectioning work in harness with each other. Usually, sequencing the thinking is less of a problem if you've got a logical system of dividing the subject you're dealing with into different 'areas of attention' in the mind. Putting a few sections into order is far easier than trying to find a good sequence through a whole mass of tiny elements. And inside each section, all you've got to think about is how to get its own elements into order. You don't have to worry too much about the way their sequence affects things in other sections. Even when you do have to consider this, the fact that you're working in sections makes it simpler.

The ability to think in logical sections and sequences even has value in organising the 'search-type' thinking of de Bono's tools. Suppose you have a difficult decision to make:

1. You might begin thinking about the situation or subject by considering your purpose with it — your reasons for needing to think about it at all. This might be the first area to explore: 'Why am I doing it?' 'What sort of result do I want?'

2. Then you might look at what you know about the situation, and develop a range of ideas to expand your thinking about what is involved. At this stage you might find useful such thinking tools as 'Information-In and Information-Out' or 'Consider All Factors'.

3. Next you might explore different ways of looking at the situation, using tools like 'Other People's Views' or 'Alternatives, Possibilities, Choices'.

4. To enable you to narrow down the range of options, you might use the 'Consequence and Sequel' tool on the more likely options, or try such an exercise as 'Plus, Minus and Interesting' or 'High-Value, Low-Value'.

5. Finally you make your decision, and work out what has to be done to implement it.

Organising the thinking

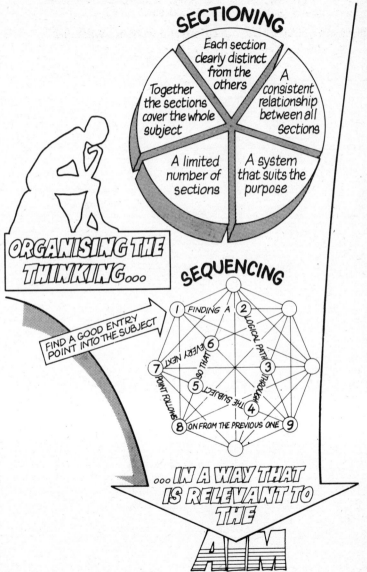

SECTIONING

Each section clearly distinct from the others

A consistent relationship between all sections

Together the sections cover the whole subject

A limited number of sections

A system that suits the purpose

ORGANISING THE THINKING...

SEQUENCING

FIND A GOOD ENTRY POINT INTO THE SUBJECT

FINDING A LOGICAL PATH THROUGH THE SUBJECT SO THAT EVERY NEXT POINT FOLLOWS ON FROM THE PREVIOUS ONE

... IN A WAY THAT IS RELEVANT TO THE AIM

15. The thinking in a decision

SHE CAN'T DECIDE WHICH DECISION TO TAKE...

Strictly speaking, all the thinking skills we've been discussing so far are part of decision-making. If you have something to decide, your first task is to understand what's involved and what range of choices you've got. The better you understand the situation and what's really important about it, the wiser your decision is likely to be. The same with your ideas about the different ways your decision could go. The better the thinking that has gone into them, the more chance you have to pick a really effective line of action. But understanding situations and thinking of alternatives doesn't actually take the decision for you. A decision is the point where you make your mind up.

However good your thinking and perception, however thorough your search for information and ideas, you can never arrive at this point knowing enough to be certain you're taking the correct decision. Perhaps there's no such thing. There are poor decisions certainly. There are also adequate decisions, good decisions, better decisions. But the only way to take the 'correct' decision would be to borrow a time-machine for a journey into the future to see if the decision had the result you hoped for. And even that wouldn't be enough. You'd have to be able to experiment with different ways of taking the decision to see if any of them produced a result even better than you'd imagined.

So you can't judge the quality of a decision by being wise after the event. How *can* you judge it? All you can do is to look at the information that was available to the decision-maker *at the time*, and the way it was used in his thinking.

Any decision you make has to be based on what you know about the present situation you're tackling and the possibilities that seem to be open to you in the future. In other words, it depends on the clues you can get to what the situation really is. It's really a question of how good you are at spotting clues and your ability to interpret them.

- The clues available to you are invariably incomplete. You can't get hold of many of the facts that are relevant. Some are simply impossible for you to find out. Others you might not have the time to obtain. You may well have to depend partly on information from other people, and they may fail to include relevant facts because they don't realise their significance. Since you don't know the facts exist, you can't ask for them.

- You may not notice many of the clues that *are* available. Perhaps you yourself fail to recognise their significance. Some may only have been available at a time when you weren't alerted to notice them — before you realised there was a decision to be taken. Some you may fail to spot because of poor observation.

- So you have to interpret the clues you *have* got. Perhaps this leads you to a faulty understanding of what is really going on. Perhaps your preconceptions get in the way — what you expect to find or how you think things ought to be. It's not uncommon for people to misread a situation from the few things they have spotted — like the conflicting accounts that witnesses of a road accident give of what actually happened. Yet each one may be absolutely convinced of the accuracy of his recollections. You have to consider different possible interpretations of the clues.

- By the time you're implementing your decision, you'll probably have further clues available that will tell you what your decision *ought* to have been. By then it's too late. When you actually take the decision, you can only try to estimate how things might change in the future, or what you might actually find in a situation you don't have any direct experience of yet. Clues are often available to indicate future trends, to calculate future probabilities, to assess future risks. If you don't try to spot them and use them, you're not making full use of the information you've got at the time.

With all this uncertainty, the 'rightness' of your decision can only be a *feeling* in your mind at the time you take it. The question is what this feeling is based on. It may be different things for different kinds of decision and different decision-makers:

A. The gut-feeling decision

Gut-feeling is an element in nearly every decision — the feelings that come from personal convictions, values, attitudes, half-forgotten bits of knowledge. Largely they are the results of subconscious mental processes, what we often call 'intuitions'. Probably such feelings are a necessary part of the confidence you need to push on, make the decision and then implement it with enough determination to make it work.

But gut-feeling decisions are the ones that are based *only* on an unsupported feeling of 'being right'. The decision-maker can't really say why he's taking the decision in the way he is — his feeling about it is all he has got. Even if he does produce reasons afterwards, he knows he's simply rationalising. They weren't the real reasons.

The trouble is that one's gut-feelings about a situation are unconsciously controlled by one's emotions. If you like to have other people's approval (and who doesn't?) you may be swayed unreasonably by what they say. Even the words they use about the situation may colour your attitude towards it. Gut-feelings can hardly be reliable for decision-making if they are affected by such flimsy suggestions. There are other snags. Alternatives may not be properly considered. Consequences and risks may not be reckoned. The gut-feeling decision is a kind of 'heads-down-and-here-we-go' jump into the unknown. It's often an easy option for those managers who are too lazy or feel too pressured to think clearly.

Despite this, gut-feeling decisions are often necessary. If you are recruiting a new member of staff for instance, your selection interviews ought to give you a lot of useful information about each candidate's suitability for the job. Your experience may help you make sense of the information you're getting and to judge its reliability. But in the final analysis, weighing people up is an art not a science. A key factor in a good selection decision is often the gut-feeling of a skilled interviewer about the candidates he has seen.

B. The 'only answer' decision

If there were ever only one answer to a situation, there would be no decision to take. Every decision assumes that there's more than one possible way to go, even if only two alternatives are considered — to go or not to go. What the 'only answer' decision-maker usually means is that none of the alternatives he has been able to think of are really workable. Every one of them would create insuperable problems. So his feeling of rightness is based on a conviction that there is no *practicable* alternative.

This is never true, or hardly ever anyway. There are always other alternatives that no one has happened to think of — yet. There's a certain arrogance in assuming that, because you haven't been able to think of other feasible options, none exist. And it's no answer to put the question to those who raise their doubts: 'then what else can *you* think of?'

Because they can't think of further possibilities on the spur of the moment proves nothing. In any case the question itself is usually asked as a form of ego-defence rather than as a true enquiry for ideas. The 'only answer' decision is a sign that the decision-maker has given up the search for fresh thought. He might better call it 'the only answer I'm willing to try to think of'.

In spite of this, for the mass of little decisions that a manager has to take there may be no point in spending valuable time trying to think up alternatives. Somewhere the search must stop. You run through the ideas that come quickly to mind, and as soon as an adequate answer presents itself that's the one you go for. It's more important to get the thing sewn up in a way that won't cause problems. But don't think it's the only answer.

The bigger decisions, the ones that have significant effects for your priorities — those are the decisions to spend exploration-time on. If any of them seem to have only one answer, go back to basics. Think further into the situation to collect a wider range of choices. Often this may not produce anything worthwhile, but at least it gives you a *chance* of finding a better solution than the one you first thought of.

C. The 'voice of experience' decision

Many decisions are the outcome of the decision-maker's feeling of familiarity with the situation he's tackling. He spots clues that lead him to assume the situation today is no different from the situation yesterday, the day before, last month, several years ago . . .

Once he knows what the situation is, that is the end of his decision-making. The decision he'll take is a foregone conclusion because it will be the same as before. He has found the tramline. The real decision was to equate the past and the present — to decide which set of rails was the appropriate one. The tramline creates the feeling of the decision's rightness.

The 'Voice Of Experience' decision actually works very well for most day-to-day questions. Many managers become highly skilful at reading a situation from a few clues. If it's a regular and frequent experience that they can look back to, the situation probably doesn't change that much each time they're faced with it. Their experience is a pretty reliable guide for interpreting clues, for reckoning what's likely to be happening, for knowing what's possible and what's not possible. It also means they can implement their decisions with the skill and assurance born of long practice. The 'voice of experience' decision-maker can look very impressive to those without the experience.

But this kind of decision-making comes unstuck when the comparisons with the past aren't valid. It's based on the idea that things don't change, 'history repeats itself' and all that. First it limits the search for clues. Once the manager has recognised a situation as comparable to something he knows, he doesn't look any further. The clues he has spotted are familiar to him — we all tend to notice familiar clues. But the unfamiliar clues are sometimes the important ones — the clues that often pass unnoticed because we're not expecting to see them, the clues that are discounted in our minds because they 'don't make sense'. Secondly it limits the search for alternatives. The manager is perfectly happy that his tramline decision is the right one in the light of the situation as he supposes it to be.

The trouble is that situations do change over time — and sometimes suddenly, often in ways that we don't expect and aren't looking for. No two situations are every *exactly* the same. They may have many features in common. But it's the features that are not the same that can make what was a reasonable decision in the past a poor one for today's circumstances. If the manager is by nature a safety-seeker, he may continue to opt for a decision that he feels has been proved to work, even though the 'proof' is illusory — coming from invalid connections with his own experience or with his knowledge of other managers who have taken the same decision. He rejects the thought that perhaps his present situation isn't the same, that his problem might have changed, that his priorities now have a different slant.

None of this denies the value of experience. It's often useful to begin looking at a situation by rummaging in one's memory for comparable situations in the past. They can throw light on the clues to look for, suggest possible ways of interpreting them, indicate lines of action to consider. But this is only a starting point for many of the important decisions. There are other questions to explore: what's different about present circumstances? What fresh clues are available and how might they be interpreted? What might be possible now that wasn't in the past?

D. The logical decision

What managers usually mean by this is that the decision-maker has thought his decision through. He has tried to use a sound reasoned approach. Facts have been gathered. Their possible implications considered. Their interpretation has been developed step by step. Alternatives and their consequences have been assessed, probabilities considered, pros and cons balanced. Of course, the decision-maker has had to make an eventual leap into the uncertainty that surrounds any decision, but his gut-feeling is supported by all the evidence of its rightness that he can muster. Sometimes he may bring forecasting techniques to bear, using his facts to extrapolate trend lines into the unknown future. The logical decision is a careful one.

On the face of it, this should be as near perfect decision-making as any human being is capable of.

The weak point in logical reasoning is that it can easily become divorced from reality. Logic works on the principle of making valid connections between the steps in a chain of reasoning: 'because A therefore B, and because B therefore C . . .' The links are all connected, but they can eventually lose contact with the real world. Indeed the logical thinker may not even start in the real world. If his 'A' is an incorrect understanding of what is actually happening, the whole edifice of thought is built on air. It has no practical value. A line of argument can be perfectly logical but simply not true in terms of actual events and practical possibilities. Mathematics is the most logical language there is. But Einstein, who should have known as much about it as anyone, once said something to the effect that the closer you get to perfect mathematical logic the further you get from reality.

The sort of manager who is particularly attracted to the idea of logical decision-making also tends to be more attracted to evidence in the form of figures and paperwork than to the evidence you get from direct observation of situations and people. He is more often a 'desk manager' than a 'walk-about manager'. Unintentionally he cuts himself off from many of the clues he needs if he is to understand the practical situation he is tackling.

There may sometimes be another snag for him. Logic lives in the 'organised thinking' department, not the 'search-type thinking' department. If his main thinking skills are indeed logical, he may not be very good at seeing different ways of understanding the situation or at thinking of any but very conventional alternatives for his decision. His decision-making will be cautious and safe. It will produce decisions that are perfectly adequate, but that don't make the most of the situations he deals with. This isn't to criticise the idea of using logic. It's to say that this shouldn't be *all* you use. If you can combine logical thinking with the skills of perception and of exploratory thinking, you've developed a very powerful range of mental skills for the decision-making you do.

E. The 'bold leap' decision

This kind of decision sometimes looks like a gut-feeling decision that's been based on a remarkably imaginative hunch. Gut-feeling certainly comes into it, but that's not the whole story. The manager who makes it knows what he's doing and why.

A properly-made 'bold leap' decision is one that has a better-than-even chance of working for all that it looks risky, though it can hardly be entirely 'safe'. The decision-maker has done his thinking about the issue he's deciding. He has looked at it from different angles, tried to see all the factors that might be relevant. He may well have considered past history more to learn what to avoid than what to follow. His exploration of alternatives hasn't been inhibited by any resistance to ideas that haven't been tried before — he has kept an open mind himself and hasn't been put off by others' criticism. *He has seen the possibility of creating a new situation with his decision.* It moves his management of his area into a new ball-game. He knows this, and that's what gives him his feeling of the rightness of the decision.

At senior levels, a bold leap is often pretty visible, and if it's successful the manager concerned gets due recognition. At lower levels it may not be so easily recognised for what it is. Where a supervisor makes such a decision, his senior may regard the issue as fairly small-time stuff and the decision itself as requiring little courage. They may not realise what it has meant to the supervisor. He had never taken a decision that way before, so he had no *direct* experience to support it.

Any manager may have few occasions to make a 'bold leap' decision. But when the opportunity comes, if he seizes it he makes one of the biggest decisions there is for him to take — and potentially one of the most productive.

However you make a decision, your own conviction of its rightness is often a crucial factor in its success. Decisions have to be implemented. The quality of the implementation can be almost as important as the quality of the decision itself — sometimes even more important. A decision that is in itself merely adequate but that is acted on with skill and the determination to *make* it work might well produce a better result than a good decision poorly executed.

The thinking in a decision

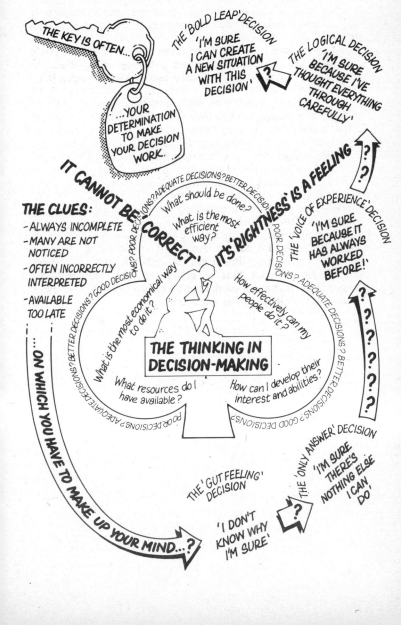

16. The core of management

Let's try to summarise the essence of what this book has been about.

At the core of every real manager's approach to his job is a certain basic orientation plus a range of skills and habits of thinking that he applies to every management question he deals with. They are directed by his sense of PURPOSE — his own purpose as a manager and his organisation's purpose for the area he has been given to manage. This sense gives him a basis for judging what does and what doesn't *contribute* to the total purpose the organisation exists to serve in society.

To make his judgements he has a set of PRIORITIES clearly established in his mind. He knows what's important about the *work* required of the set-up he's managing; he is conscious of the value of *money* it costs to run it; he respects the needs and interests of the *people* who are in it. He recognises how these priorities interact and conflict with each other. To resolve the

177

conflicts he has *ordered his priorities* in a way that matches the needs of his organisation and his level in it.

His role is to MAKE THINGS HAPPEN. He does this in two main ways. He makes *decisions*. He *communicates* with others to collect the information on which to base his decisions and to get them acted on with good will.

Many of his key decisions are about his DELEGATION to his subordinates, which governs practically everything they do as employees of his organisation. He accepts *responsibility* for their actions — and encourages them to accept responsibility too. To the extent that they do so, he gives them a part of his own *authority* to make decisions and expects them to use it. He holds them *accountable* to himself for their use of this decision-making authority.

He uses a variety of MANAGEMENT SKILLS. Skills in *planning* whatever is to be done and in *organising* his resources to make the best use of them; skills in providing *leadership* for his people; skills in knowing what is going on — the skills of *controlling*; skills in *developing* the effectiveness of his operation and his people. Although he shares many of these skills with people in other occupations, it is the way he blends them together in his thinking and behaviour that creates his particular abilities as a manager.

All these skills of his depend on another kind of skill — his basic ability in THINKING. He refuses to let ego-defences or ignorance of things that are relevant to his management, trap his mind in tram-lines when he should be steering it in more positive and constructive directions. He tries to keep himself widely informed. He persistently practises the skills of thinking on the situations and problems that confront him. In his decision-making he is alert for clues and aware of the judgements he is basing on them. His decisions are appropriate to *all* the circumstances he is aware of.

If you're that good, you're a real manager.